CONTENTS

World-proof Your Kids

Raising Children Unstained by the World

Timothy A. Sisemore

Dr Timothy A. Sisemore is one of America's leading child and adolescent Christian psychologists. He is the Clinal Professor of Psychology and Counselling at the Psychological Studies Institute. He maintains a clinical practice at the Chattanooga Bible Institute Counseling Center and has been published in Professional Psychology Research & Practice, The Journal for Christian Educators and the Journal of Psychology & Christianity. Ruth Sisemore is his wife and vitally helps Tim translate theory into practice!

© Timothy A. Sisemore

ISBN 1-84550-275-2
ISBN 978-1-84550-275-1

10 9 8 7 6 5 4 3 2 1

Published in 2007
by
Christian Focus Publications Ltd.,
Geanies House, Fearn, Tain,
Ross-shire, IV20 1TW, Great Britain
www.christianfocus.com

Cover Design by Moose77.com
Printed and Bound by CPD, Wales

1

THE FRUIT OF THE SPIRIT
IN A BARREN LAND

My schooling as a psychologist didn't prepare me for this. I came out of my training ready to serve children who had the classical psychological disorders. I knew Christians could be depressed or anxious at times, and I was keen to help these families. I envisioned caring families united in their desire to ease their children's suffering. In my naiveté, I thought this would be the heart of my counseling practice. I was, in short, wrong.

I quickly learned that most Christian families who came to me for help were fighting for the spiritual lives of their children. The same anger I saw in youth from unbelieving families engrossed teens from Christian homes. Their faith was not important or strong enough to discourage their pursuit of the fleeting pleasures of sex, alcohol, rebellion, or other 'pleasures' of the world. Young children were demanding and disobedient, not the least bit shy to embarrass their parents in public, to pressure them to buy the latest toy, gadget, or yet another candy bar. These little ones often did not believe they had a problem; their parents had the problem because they wanted to control their children's behavior. Many of these children believed they were entitled to whatever they wanted and did not need be subject to anyone. It somehow seemed as though being from a Christian family did not make a difference any more.

I was also surprised that these families turned rather quickly to me, a psychologist. The culture has trained these parents that any uncomfortable behaviors or emotions must be something medical. Very often they are already convinced that their children need medication to straighten them out. Others seek a diagnosis so the problems have an explanation, or so the parents have an excuse. Let me be clear here. I believe children can and do suffer from mental disorders. Our brains are fallen, too, and can go awry. My point is that Christians should be slow to 'medicalize' problems the Bible calls sin. For example, the Ten Commandments actually forbid several 'symptoms' of Oppositional Defiant Disorder. Lying and stealing thus reflect a psychiatric disorder, not sins against a Holy God. This is a dangerous change in our interpretation. It means Christian parents may bypass parental discipline and the church to seek professional help.

How can this be? Most Christian parents genuinely care about their children and long for them to grow to be faithful to our Lord. We have more Christian parenting books than ever (including mine!). We have Christian radio and television programs led by sincere groups such as James Dobson's Focus on the Family, and a wide assortment of Christian parenting products from books to DVDs to music. We have enticing and exciting youth programs in many of our churches. So what is wrong? Why do Christian children live and act so much like those who do not know Christ?

Our children are being stained by the world. The world is no longer 'out there', an enemy distant and visible. Our warfare is no longer conventional, but more like the fight against terrorism with the lines between 'us' and 'them' not so clearly drawn as our enemy is not making itself openly known. Our enemy maliciously penetrates the borders of our churches and even our homes. The media brings the message of the world into our living rooms while secular educators teach it in the classroom. Churches, seeking to be 'relevant', adapt the marketing practices of the world to make the gospel attractive, yet in so doing water down the gospel. This subtle invasion has met with inadequate resistance by many believers, and gone almost unnoticed by others. It is easy for modern Christians in rich areas of the world to even forget there is an enemy because we naively equate prosperity with God's blessing. The staining influences of the world have infiltrated Christendom with stealth and efficiency. Even when we do fight back, we may often do so with little understanding of what we are fighting for...and against. It is time to rise and defend our churches and particularly our children. It is paramount for us as believers to return to the offensive in our parenting and nurture of our children. We serve a Risen King, and we must actively pursue a hunger and thirst for his righteousness in our lives and the lives of our children, a righteousness characterized by the fruit of God's Spirit. Only then we will reclaim our churches, families, and children, and again be unstained by the world.

Stains Come Easily

James 1: 27[1] teaches us that 'Religion that is pure and undefiled before God and the Father is this: to visit orphans and widows in their affliction, and to keep oneself unstained by the world.' It is the goal of every Christian parent to have their children grow into 'pure and undefiled' religion. The same is true of church leaders, youth directors, and teachers of children. Indeed, the entire church of Jesus Christ strives to demonstrate such pure religion, and to raise her children to embrace it.

James' definition of pure religion challenges us. I wonder how we might have defined it. Many of us would say pure religion consists of a shortlist of don'ts—don't watch certain movies, don't take drugs, don't miss church services, don't smoke, and so forth. These are comfortable, for they focus on specific external behaviors that make it relatively easy to have 'pure religion'. Or we might define it more positively by certain dos. 'Pure religion' would then be that I read my Bible everyday, I give thanks before every meal, I pray for my family, I listen to Christian music. This is a little more difficult, but doable. Or maybe we might boldly combine aspects of the two. Still, these are fairly convenient and make us feel too readily that we have obtained our goal.

James also lists positive and negative means to the end goal of godliness, but he does so in a much more demanding

7

way. The context of this passage tells us true religion consists in doing what the word of God teaches, not merely hearing it. James details what this looks like. Much could be said of the positive ministry to widows and orphans, especially when the church too easily focuses on power rather than weakness (contrast 1 Cor. 1: 18–2: 5). But, our focus is to be on what it means to be 'unstained' by the world.

The Greek word used here for 'unstained', *aspilos*, occurs only a few times in the Bible. In 1 Peter 1: 19 the term refers to 'a lamb without blemish or spot,' suggesting purity, and 1 Timothy 6: 14, exhorts us 'to keep the commandment unstained and free from reproach until the appearing of our Lord Jesus Christ.' Finally, 2 Peter 3: 14 urges believers to be found 'without spot' when the Lord returns. The common theme is purity from sin and defilement, with the implication that we are 'stained' as believers when impurity taints our obedience or when the earthly impinges on our walk with Christ.

We most commonly think of stains on clothing. We experience a special anxiety when we wear a white shirt or blouse to dinner with a friend and realize spaghetti is on the menu. Transporting the splattery sauce from its resting-place to our mouths challenges our skills. If we merely sit and look at the plate, it is easy to remain unstained. But when we interact with the food, preventing it from getting on our clothing requires care and effort.

A more pertinent example is watching children on the church lawn after an Easter service. Parents with quiet horror gaze at their children, dressed in neatly pressed pants or dainty pastel dress, as a game of tag unfolds on the newly mown grass. One minor misstep, one slight error and a determined stain of grass will mar the loveliest Easter frock. Grass is all around them, and awaits even the briefest opportunity to make its indelible mark on the purest clothing. Possibly we might imagine another youngster picking up a clump of grass or mud and flinging it maliciously at our child. The world does not lie passively about us, but attacks us with fiery malice.

This image resonates with biblical implication. In Revelation (3: 4–5; 4: 4; 7: 9) the righteous wear white clothing, whereas those who sinned in the church of Sardis (by not doing the works of righteousness and not demonstrating the 'pure

8

religion' of James) have 'soiled their garments'. They will not walk in white clothing. These texts do not suggest one loses one's salvation, yet they challenge us to make our 'calling and election sure' (2 Pet. 1: 10). We are to be diligent in our own lives, by God's grace, to be unstained by the world. It is also our honored obligation to raise children, in our homes and churches, who stand with us against the world's readiness to stain. Avoiding stain is not just avoiding contact with the world, but dodging the incessant efforts of our spiritual enemies to harm us (Eph. 6: 10–18).

What are the 'stains' of the world? We will spend much of this book looking at these, but first, let us note a few themes. Our pictures of staining above are instructive as they show the difficulty of being near something that can stain without letting it get to us. We are to be 'in the world but not of it'. The monks missed this point as they retreated from the world. As noble as their intentions were, it is admittedly easier to remain unstained if you have no contact with the source of the stain. This is not to say there are no temptations in solitude (recall Jesus was in the wilderness when tempted), but this does reduce the danger of exposure to the world.

In our day, the world touches on our lives in countless ways that even believers of old, outside of monasteries, would find threatening. If we look back a mere 100 years into history, we see how much less contact families had with the world than we do now. Families interacted in communities, though often these communities shared the Christian faith more than today. Men were exposed to the secular world in the workplace, women in the market place. Children, in contrast, were relatively protected. Homes were sanctuaries in many ways. Parents bought the only books and magazines in the house. There were no televisions, computers, radios, or DVD players. Children were educated at home, or in the local school which was often explicitly Christian in orientation. They talked, but of games and friends, not of the latest movie or music. Exposure to the staining influence of the world was limited. Childhood was described as a time of innocence.

It is no longer so. Early twenty-first century Western culture sees itself obligated to let even young children know about sex, violence, and consumerism, as though they are children's rights, and innocence a deprivation of these 'rights'. The media that have brought the world closer in many ways have increased the ease of being stained. From the time children are old enough to say their first words, television commercials preach materialism inside our homes, potentially opposing the teaching of biblical generosity by faithful parents.

While many Christian parents take great care selecting which movies or programs their young charges are exposed to, they miss the significant acculturation effected by even seemingly 'harmless' shows. Mass marketing pressures even very young children to have the latest 'look' in clothing. A recent television children's program depicted as a part of the fairy tale the story of a lady-in-waiting who was pregnant and needed to marry quickly to cover her situation, extolling the message that love is more powerful than law. Many children's programs portray violence as humorous and justified, while video games push the limits of our tolerance, the latest ones including the portrayal of cannibalism.

The secularization of schools stains our children with the unchristian idea that all of life can be explained without reference to God or religion. (I write this during Thanksgiving week in the United States where we celebrate the pilgrims' coming to America and inviting newly-made American friends to join in giving thanks to God for his provision. Despite the religious motive of these people coming to these shores, and the explicit giving of thanks to the God of the Bible, American schoolchildren now learn only that this was about a 'spirit' of thankfulness with no role for religious faith. Ahead no longer lies Advent or the Christmas season, but the 'holiday season' where one might be sacked for wishing a customer 'Merry Christmas' rather than 'Happy Holidays'.)

Moreover, Christian parents are more caught up in the ways of the world than we like to think as the culture invades our lives and homes. As we are distracted from our biblical focus, we may appear lost in the (post)modern world, and thus susceptible to being stained by it. If that is the case, how will we guide our children aright through the times? We must, then, become more alert to the dangers of the world in which we live, and raise our children more intentionally for Christ.

Families Inadvertently Stained

Just as I don't want spaghetti on my shirt, families do not seek out worldliness. Part of the tragedy is that no genuinely Christian family wants to be stained by the world, nor do they wish this upon their children. Many parents succumb to blind spots that leave them, and their children, vulnerable to the unchristian influences of our day. Let us consider a few examples.

THE DISILLUSIONED FAMILY

A common recipe for parenting is that if you give children what they want, make life pleasant, and bolster their self-esteem, they will turn out fine. This stems from humanistic reasoning that denies the sinful nature of children, yet Christian parents often adopt it as the best parenting philosophy. It is even found in some Christian parenting literature. After all, children are sweet and innocent, and ancient ideas of their being sinful are insults to children. Meticulously these parents search out opportunities for their children to be on the best sports teams, go to the best schools, have the best gadgets, attend the most exciting church, and hang out with the most enviable friends. Doing such, it is assumed, will produce joy and satisfaction leading to grateful obedience. After all, isn't being Christian all about grace? Instead, the beleaguered parents moan, 'But why does he act that way? We've done everything for him!' These parents often place their children in expensive Christian schools and take them to church regularly. Yet, the stains of materialism and social climbing sabotage their efforts. The Christian faith is not intended to give us an advantage in reaching the goals those around us share. Rather, it focuses us on different goals altogether: God and his glory. As a result, these children conclude that what matters is their immediate gratification, and they are angry when it is not provided for them. The ideas of their sinfulness and need for forgiveness are alien to these little ones.

THE DISTRACTED FAMILY

This family is caught in the flow of the hustle and bustle of contemporary life. Father works long hours to provide, while mother runs the family shuttle hither and yon for sports practices, lessons, and church youth functions. Many times both parents work and trade out the chauffeuring responsibilities. This group arrives at church only to disperse. Each member scurries (for this group is most often running a bit late) to his or her own Sunday School class. After that the younger children reunite with their parents briefly for the first part of the worship service before they are escorted off to children's church. The teens have their own service designed to suit their adolescent tastes. Once home, it is each one for themselves given the many activities to which they are obligated, and it is a rare event for them to sit down to a meal at home (though they would really like to when their schedule allows). There is never enough time for the distracted family as they try to do everything they can, and all in the Name of Christ. All of their activities are wholesome, but something is missing.

Children from the distracted family learn little of true Christian fellowship, despite spending most of their time around believers. Faith becomes a to-do list of things to do before bedtime. Lost is the biblical notion of time alone with God, of quiet times together as family, of reflection on what this is all about anyway. Martha, not Mary, is the role model for this clan. These children may tire from the manic pace and seek consolation with friends who just 'hang out' and have few expectations of each other, leading to underachievement and passivity. Others may continue their frenetic pace with little thought for the God they allegedly serve. The stain of the pace of modern life claims many of these children in differing ways.

THE DISCIPLINARIAN FAMILY

This is a common pattern characterized by parents who are zealous that their children do right. If you meet their children, they are likely polite and well-mannered. They regularly attend church meetings. You are unlikely to see children from these families acting rudely in public. Even small affronts meet with consequences in these homes in the parents' diligence to keep their children from sin. These children have learned that to do wrong is to earn the wages of the sin. The parents know the danger of sin, and steer their children well clear of it as much as they can. Not that this is bad, of course. But simply focusing on discipline will not lead to inward godliness and purity of heart.

A primary problem with such families often is the lack of love. While abundant punishments may gain obedience, it can foster resentment and the anger that fathers in particular must not provoke (Eph. 6: 4). Often as these children mature, they become disillusioned with the faith, assuming God is like their earthly parents, quick to punish and slow to forgive. The world becomes attractive because these children see little in the Christian faith that attracts them. Their parents have failed to give these little ones a vision of the glory and goodness of God

THE DEDICATED FAMILY

These folks are the most sincere of all about their faith. They are faithful to church, pray for their children, and seek God in their lives. They have family devotions and serve others in the community in the name of Christ. In their spare time, the parents study their Bibles and read Christian books. Admittedly, though, many meals are eaten in front of the television, and renting movies is a favorite pastime. The men and boys gather round for raucous times watching their favorite sports teams on the TV, and take in the games live when they can. Catch these folks after church and they'll be chatting with friends about the latest movie or game, or catching up on the latest celebrity gossip.

The subtle 'stain' here is that for all their Christian commitment, the dedicated family is more a part of the culture than they would like to think. Oh, they don't watch sex or violence-laden movies, or listen to music with vile lyrics, but they *do* watch a lot of movies and buy a lot of music. They are very much a part of the consumer culture, and the power and attraction of the culture are sirens calling the children away from their faith commitments to the immediate, transient gratifications of modern life. It is almost a schizophrenic lifestyle: the sincere devotion to the faith being compartmentalized to leave room for indulgence in the entertainments of the culture. The latter may be done in the name of Christian freedom to enjoy God's creation. Often parents in dedicated families grieve intensely as they struggle to hold on as their teens drift away from God, understanding little about how this came about.

These families are, of course, stereotypes. We may see a little of ourselves in each, or much of ourselves in one of them. Still, they illustrate the variety of ways of coping with modern life that can leave our children polluted. Such short descriptions miss the crafty ways the stain of the world impacts believers. We will come to know these ways better in the pages that lie ahead.

Unstained Fruit

Return with me, if you will, to our Easter scene on the church grounds. The parents of the romping children do not have as their goal merely to keep the children from staining their clothes. Rather, the stains are shunned because they hinder a higher goal. These parents are eager for their little ones to be dressed in their finest and look their best on the day where we celebrate the new life that is ours in Christ through his resurrection. It would not do to be unstained while wearing play clothes. Purity and beauty are the goals, and these are incompatible with stains.

Even so, it is not the goal of Christian parents merely to be unstained by the world, but we avoid the stains in pursuit of holiness of life. We want our children to grow to be like Christ, and we know the world will hinder this goal. In a previous work[2] I defined the goal of parenting and the nurture of children in the church to be 'to raise children through guidance and discipline to faith in Christ, so that they glorify him in every area of their lives, eventually passing the faith on to their children.' Note the positive cast of this goal as it echoes the *Westminster Confession*. We pray not that our children merely do not curse or take drugs. Rather, we seek the grace of God that they will live to his glory and to enjoy him forever. We look past the psychological goal of children with healthy personalities and aspire for our children instead to have godly *character*.

There are numerous ways one might be more specific about what such glorifying of God looks like in daily life. It might be called being sanctified (1 Thess. 5: 23), or exhibiting the qualities of the Beatitudes (Matt. 5: 2–12), or having the mind of Christ (1 Cor. 2: 16). But one of the clearest outlines of what the God-glorifying Christian life should look like is the fruit of the Spirit that Paul lists in Galatians 5: 22–3. This list is in specific contrast to the desires of the flesh (Gal. 5: 16–17) which are among the 'stains' of the world. We avoid gratifying the flesh most fully when we walk by the Spirit, and walking by the Spirit is characterized by his fruit.

The surest way to avoid our children's being stained by the world, and of growing to glorify God in all their lives, is to guide them to walk in the Spirit and display his fruit in their lives. Conversely, one can easily argue that the devil, eager to neutralize the rising generation of Christians, would work overtime to prevent such fruit from appearing. If our enemy can mire our precious children down by staining them with works of the flesh, he figures to reduce their fruitfulness and thus keep them from glorifying God as they ought.

In light of this, we do well to consider the fruit of the Spirit as goals for our children, and to examine the ways of the world as they would hinder these fruit. Our children will be best kept unstained by the world if we…and they…are actively seeking God's fruit in their lives. The purpose of this book is to help Christians who care for children, be you parents, grandparents, teachers, ministers, counselors, or church leaders, to guide them into the blessed fruit of the Spirit. In so doing, we will examine the nature of the fruit and how it is manifested (ch. 2) and contrast this with the works of the flesh (ch. 3) before examining each fruit individually (chs. 4–13). In each of these, we will carefully consider how the fruit can be displayed in the lives of young people, and explore the contemporary threats to our children that make it more difficult for our children to bear each fruit. We will consider for each of the fruit some specific ways parents can nurture their children toward that fruit, and reflect on ways those in the church can support these children and their families in their fight for faith and fruit. We will conclude with a look at some ways the church can rally to the aid of parents fighting for the spiritual lives of their children in our postmodern world.

No, my psychological training did not prepare me for this battle for our children. Yet, it did equip me to see dangers in the culture and in family and church life that are harming our children and threatening the next generation of believers. In this study, we seek to draw upon the Word of God, training and experience, research, and our burden for God's covenant children to offer reflections and guidance for others who care for the children of the church, and those outside as well. Let us prayerfully consider how we might seek God's grace to love, nurture, educate, and shepherd children who glorify God by bearing the fruit of his Spirit, and in so doing embody pure religion and are unstained by the world.

As we begin this study, let me offer some suggestions to the reader. You may choose simply to read through the book at your leisure. I suggest, though, that you consider a slower, more deliberate approach. Consider taking one chapter per week (or even per month if you are able). Make that chapter a matter of prayer for you and your family. Possibly study the verses discussed in detail, or read further on the topic covered. As mentioned, most chapters end with some suggestions for application. Prayerfully consider them, then choose one to implement. One challenge of our society is that it discourages acting on what we read or see. This might be your first change: be intentional about responding to what you read and what I pray God's Spirit will use to prompt you to change. You might be able to put more than one suggestion per chapter into practice, and that would be wonderful. But slow change is often the best change. I strongly recommend that couples read this together so each can encourage the other and cooperate to make important changes. You might consider reading it with another couple for accountability and prayer support, or even in a small group study to broaden the base of spiritual encouragement.

Even now, take a few minutes to seek God's face. Ask him, by the power of his Holy Spirit, to guide you as you read and to strengthen you to act so your children might be servants of Christ, and unstained by the world.

2

FOR PARENTS OF PRODIGALS

Darrin was a handful.[1] This young boy was as impulsive as they come. Certainly he was bright, but that only meant he had more creative impulses to pursue. Despite his desire to do right, he found himself in trouble frequently at school, church, and at home. Here's the irony: Darrin's mother worked as hard at getting him to obey as any parent I've worked with. She actively cooperated with his teacher and followed up at home when he misbehaved at school. With his father, she developed an elaborate system of rewards and punishments for his behavior at home. The family not only sought my help, they followed my advice with rigor. Still, he was a handful.

As frustrating as this was to his parents, the response of people at their church made it worse. Rather than support and encouragement, Darrin's family faced criticism and put-downs. Most commonly, these comments were something like, 'If only you used such and such technique like *I* do, his problems would go away.' Or, 'You should read such and such a book, and that'll tell you how to fix it.' Or worse, 'Maybe God isn't pleased with you, and this is the result. You need to pray more for your son and find the sin in your life that may underlie the problems you have.'

Darrin, it turns out, had a fairly serious case of attention problems that were resistant to most everything that was tried. He finally improved, but only due to the faithful and patient perseverance of his family. Common disciplinary approaches that worked with most children didn't faze him. The result was the parents felt alienated at church and like failures in their faith. By God's grace they fought through their discouragement, but the struggle lasted for years.

Alice was a pleasant teenager who was open about her views. Her parents were devout believers who kept her in church and even enrolled her in a Christian school to minimize the world's influence on her. This didn't work. Alice rather flatly told me she respected her parents as Christians and did not consider them hypocrites, but she rejected the demands of Christ on her behavior. 'I may become a Christian some day, but right now I want to have my fun and do what I want.' So, she experimented with alcohol and sex, eschewing the efforts of her parents to control her behavior. They suffered greatly, wondering where God was in their daughter's rebellion and rejection of the faith. The family's church, sadly like most, was one where giving an impression of godliness was more important than being godly, so the family's entire problem was ignored and the parents found little support or encouragement there.

I share the stories of Darrin and Alice for the sake of readers who may identify with them. While the focus of this book is primarily to help prevent problems and promote the fruit of the Spirit, it will most likely also find its way into the hands of parents of prodigals. These parents, or others who know and love a prodigal, may only dream of seeing the fruit of the Spirit in the life of the child or young person they love. For these dear brothers and sisters, and for those who might offer consolation and help to them, I offer this chapter. My hope is that I might provide some insight into why some children of believers stray from the faith and provide some suggestions of ways to cope with these painful situations.

The Biblical Backdrop

In my previous book, *Of Such is the Kingdom*[2], I detailed a biblical understanding of the nature of children before God, so I will only offer a brief summary of the relevant points here. God created man in his own image (Gen. 1: 26), yet that image was tarnished when Adam sinned. Today's children bear a distorted image and thus have a tendency to use their gifts in self-serving rather than God-serving ways. The presence of sin in their lives makes this worse. Christians have traditionally believed in the doctrine of original sin, the notion that sin is present in individuals from the moment of conception (e.g. Ps. 51: 5). Sins are not simply specific acts children (or adults, for that matter) commit, but the specific acts that flow from a corrupted heart, inclined to serve itself in rebellion against God. This is why children need discipline: they will go astray in ways that are not only wrong, but that are self-destructive, if not shaped by the correction of loving parents.

Christian traditions vary on whether or not a child must come to have a specific conversion experience. Much of the Reformed tradition, from which I write, views children as heirs of the covenant promises of God, placing them in a special relationship with the family of God. Views range from assuming children of believing parents will be saved to thinking that being raised by Christians makes little difference to the likelihood of a conversion experience. One strand of the tradition[3] maintains that the covenant promises mean that Christian parents can expect their children to be saved so long as the parents live faithful lives themselves and raise them in godly ways.

Without debating these issues here, let us assume that children raised by believing parents and who enjoy the benefits of the covenant community of the church, undoubtedly enjoy blessings children of unbelievers miss. This means that it is at least more likely that children of believers will come to faith than is true for children of unbelievers, though God is still sovereign over who comes to faith (as Jesus makes clear in his high priestly prayer in John 17, see particularly verse 24). There is a strong link between the faithfulness of parents and the faith of their children. Thus the wonderful passage in Deuteronomy 6 expects and even commands godly guidance. Possibly the strongest case for this link stems from Proverbs 22: 6, 'Train up a child in the way he should go; even when he is old he will not depart from it.' Whether this means that a child's departing from the way directly implies that the parents did not train him up properly is a subject of considerable debate, a debate also beyond the scope of our purposes here. Proper parenting undoubtedly is important, yet we must recognize that the Bible gives numerous accounts of wayward children that cannot easily be dismissed as entirely the fault of the parents.

Let me summarize. Children are born in sin and thus affected by a sinful nature. This requires the discipline of parents to control it, but the grace of God is needed to overcome it through regeneration. Children born into Christian homes have many advantages, and these give great hope to parents that their children will be saved. Believing parents bear a great responsibility to train their children in the faith and this is under no circumstances to be neglected. Usually, the failure of parents to properly train their children in the faith bears responsibility for children who are worldly and do not live faithful Christian lives. However, I would like to suggest there are some situations that offer consolation to parents of prodigals.

Situations that Challenge Christian Parents

BIOLOGICALLY-BASED CHALLENGES

One consequence of sin entering the world is that disease exists and the gene pool is defiled so children may inherit deformities from their parents. Many of these are physical. Recall Jesus saying neither the blind man *nor his parents* had sinned to cause his blindness (John 9: 2–3, though this does not rule out the possibility of that being true sometimes). Some parents face challenges with their children that cannot be traced to their own wrongdoings. Down's syndrome is a case in point. The basis of this genetic disorder is well understood, and it not only causes physical differences, it also renders the children who have it intellectually challenged. Parents have no control over this, yet it leaves children unable to understand the gospel. Other genetic disorders may make children even more profoundly retarded, and unable to grasp anything of the content of the faith. These are sometimes accompanied by behavior problems since these children lack the cognitive abilities to understand and control their behavior. They learn very slowly, and sometimes not at all. We believe that God extends saving mercy to at least some of such children while not directly holding parents responsible for their behavior and lack of 'faith'. God still calls parents to be faithful, but obviously their obedience in caring for such children will look a bit different from when children are normal.

This principle extends to children who have suffered brain damage from seizures, an accident, or from some other cause. This would also apply to children who experience learning disabilities. The brain is easily the most complex organ of our bodies, and it should not seem strange that it can experience subtle malformations just like any other organ given the effects of sin on creation in general. These malformations impact our mental processes and behavior, and are assumed to account for learning disabilities and the problems in understanding and communicating they produce. It is then a short step to include other brain-based problems such as severe inattention and lack of behavioral or emotional control. We must admit that often these are just sinful misbehavior, but the logic remains: if areas of the brain that control these functions are not intact, problems will follow that could include what we call sin. My point is *not* to excuse sin, but to allow that for some children, controlling behavior and emotion is much more challenging than for others, and parents of such children need encouragement and support (assuming they are indeed seeking to be faithful in their parenting).

BIBLICAL EXAMPLES

Children may well suffer for the sins of their parents. This truth is evident in the Ten Commandments, where God makes clear that he is 'a jealous God, visiting the iniquity of the fathers on the children to the third and the fourth generation of those who hate me, but showing steadfast love to thousands of those who love me and keep my commandments' (Exod. 20: 5b–6). One need look no further than the fate of David's illegitimate child (2 Sam. 12: 15–23). Yet, his marriage to Bathsheba produced a godly king, Solomon. David was a man of God, but fathered

21

the prototypical rebellious child, Absalom. I recall a little six-year-old boy with whom I worked who was born with AIDS due to his mother's using tainted needles to take drugs while she was pregnant. Certainly he paid for her sin with his health.

Again, while the overwhelming trend is that godly parents produce godly children, there are clear exceptions. Even Adam and Eve, despite their sin, raised Abel who was faithful to God, yet also nurtured Cain whose weaker faith led to his being a murderer and then an exile (Gen. 4: 1–16). Long before disciplinary approaches were at issue, Isaac and Rebekah learned their twin sons had different destinies. In Genesis 25: 23, the Lord tells Rebekah of the future conflict between her boys and that the younger would serve the elder. This is even more bluntly stated by God, 'Jacob have I loved, but Esau I hated' (Rom. 9: 13, citing Mal. 1: 2, 3). Granted Rebekah was a bit manipulative of Isaac's blessing, yet her twins' destiny was sealed before her manipulations. God takes parental faithfulness into account, but the use of the story in Romans is to show God's providence, not the impact of the parents' behavior.

The story of the kings of Judah and Israel detailed in 2 Kings and 2 Chronicles is relevant because of how many times godly kings begat successors who were sinful, and idolatrous kings passed power on to sons who were faithful to God. Though details are scanty in some of these accounts, it is plain that faithful fathers sometimes had rebellious children. In many cases, the behavior of these kings was compared to David as their 'father'. For example, Ahaz 'did not do what was right in the eyes of the Lord, as his father David had done' (2 Chr. 28: 1). The tenor of this comment is that Ahaz was responsible for his moral failure given the godly example of David, even more interesting in light of David being a 'mixed bag' of frequently obeying God in his life, yet sinning grievously on some occasions.

This raises a final point: how godly is godly? Since most of us do not believe in perfect sanctification this side of heaven, no parents are perfect. As I sometimes joke with parents I work with, not being Catholic, I don't even believe Mary was a perfect parent! It is therefore difficult to say how 'good' you must be to expect your children to follow in kind. Let it suffice to say that each of us, as followers of Jesus, should seek God's grace to be as faithful as possible to his calling as parents or caregivers to children, trusting him for saving grace and obedience in our children. Knowing we are sincerely seeking him, we look to him in prayer and faith for the well-being of our children.

CHILDREN AS VICTIMS OF LIFE

There are several scenarios that may leave sincere Christian parents with challenging children, despite their best intentions to raise them faithfully.

Adoption is a wonderful ministry to which many Christian couples are called. Believers are known for taking into their families unwanted children from near home and abroad. Yet, sometimes this is done a bit naively, with these couples believing that they will take a child into their home and fix all of her problems. This overlooks two important things. First, the role of genetics that we've already discussed comes into play. But moreover, research now tells us that considerable portions of personality traits are inherited. Consider, then, who gives children up for adoption? These are most often women who impulsively got pregnant, who had problems such that they could not raise their child, who were neglectful or abusive, or were in poverty. These may mean they pass on some questionable genes, and the impact on these children cannot be minimized. But second, this often means that adopted children come from backgrounds that impact their adjustment in troubling ways. Poor prenatal care increases the risk for learning and behavioral problems. The same can be said for poor nutrition, lack of caring parents during formative early years, and the adversities faced in orphanages abroad and foster care closer to home.

And what of parents who began raising children before they became Christians? These children had formative experiences that were not under the nurture of Christ through the church and godly parents. Such situations call for special grace as Christian care replaces unspiritual parenting practices. The plight of parents whose spouses left them is also a particular challenge. Divorce is sadly very common, and increases the risk of psychological problems for the children who go through it. Even if the remaining parent is a believer, there is often the contradictory influence of the other parent, the sense of betrayal the child may experience, and often a drop in financial status forcing the remaining parent (usually the mother) to go to work. I have spoken with many parents, divorced against their wills, who lament their inability to provide the 'ideal' Christian home environment for their children due to their life circumstances. This is tragic enough, but their frustration is exacerbated when they turn to the church and feel estranged rather than welcomed and understood.

With so many different Christian parenting books and programs available, I believe many well-meaning believing parents end up with troubled children because they followed a program that was not truly biblical or wise. This is generally done in good faith, and can embitter parents who thought they were doing the 'Christian' thing when they were misled. Here again, the church plays a vital role in giving parents biblical guidance on raising children in the faith.

Finally, we must admit that we are living when culture is more subtle and yet more powerful than in most times past. No longer do school systems support Christian values. 'Pop' culture has become so common that it has almost erased more genteel and 'civilized' ways of being in community. This culture invades our homes through multiple media and targets our children directly. As we will see, children are no longer protected, but seen as efficient targets for reaching the parents' pocketbooks. Just as it is easier to stumble when climbing a mountain than when walking down the street, surely it is more understandable to fail as parents in a hostile culture like ours compared to times when the Christian faith was more a part of mainstream society and values.

I hope this discussion has shown that children, born in sin, easily go astray without proper guidance, and even sometimes despite it. While most children owe much of their worldliness to their parents, there are many parents who are seeking faithfully to follow God and still have rebellious children. Let us as fellow believers be swift to care, and slower to judge, sharing with believing parents a longing that children follow the Lord.

Why Children of Christians Leave the Faith

Considerable research has been done on why children leave the faith of their parents. While research by its nature does not consider God's role in events, it sheds light on the outworking of God's principles for how we should act, and thus can help us understand what is happening and, to an extent, what we are doing wrong.

A major recent study in the United States[4] suggests that Mormons, an offshoot of the true Christian faith, do a better job of keeping their children in their faith from generation to generation than do evangelical Christians. For example, of teenagers in the Latter Day Saints tradition, about 75% say their religious beliefs are very similar to those of their parents. Compare this to conservative Protestants where the numbers drop to about 45%. Even though both groups overall keep about 86% of their children in the faith overall, it appears the Mormons do a better job of passing on the content and practices of their faith to their children. While 43% of Mormon teens see their faith as important in shaping their daily lives, this holds true for only 29% of conservative Protestant teenagers. Stated inversely, this tells us that over two-thirds of conservative Christian teens in the US do not see their faith as being important in their daily lives. One assumes this is not too different from other Western countries, and this is cause for concern. It appears we not only are failing to teach our children the faith in such a way that it shapes their lives, but we are failing to teach them how to discern truth from error, yielding to the vague spiritualities of the age. We might strongly disagree with the Mormons on their doctrine, but they seem to do a better job of teaching it to their children and working it into their lives than we do. Here is a call to Christian parents to be more intentional in teaching the faith to our children, and to churches to take more seriously the importance of Christian education.

Tom Bisset[5] cites four major reasons children of Christian parents leave the faith. (I should note that the idea here is *not* that they lose their salvation, but that genuine believing faith has not taken root in their lives.) His first is because their troubling questions about the faith go unanswered. Teenagers have a history of asking difficult questions. In my counseling practice, I find it remarkable how many adolescents like to talk 'philosophy' about the meaning of life, the way things are, and what God has to do with it all. Sadly, it seems many of these teens find little other place to discuss their questions.

Most church youth group meetings intend to entertain more than educate as we think we have to look and sound as much like the world as possible for teens to come. This flows from the naïve idea that teens love the world as it is and wouldn't be interested in Christianity if it didn't look like the Western world of the early 21st Century. I fear that our young people take our silence on important issues to mean that we can't answer their questions and our failure to offer them anything more substantial than a good time as a sign that our faith has little of depth to offer.

Where does this failure to proclaim Christian truth and answer challenging questions leave us? With what used to be called syncretism, a blending of ideas of the Christian faith with the spiritual beliefs of the surrounding culture. Christian Smith[6] reports that among American conservative Protestant teens, 33% maybe or definitely believe in reincarnation, 33% believe in astrology, 31% in communicating with the dead, and 21% in psychics and fortune tellers. Contemporary Christian music may provide an alternate form of entertainment for our children, but we are failing horribly in our efforts to provide a truly Christian education. Our families and our churches stand indicted on this count.

The second reason Bisset found for our children to leave the faith was a discovery that their faith was not working for them. Does this mean God is unfaithful? As Paul would say, may it never be! What, then, is the problem? Based on my experience, I believe that we fail to communicate to our children the true nature of the faith. This is a core argument for this entire book. We 'sell' the faith as a way of being happy while defining 'happy' in the same way the world does. Become a Christian and you won't have problems, you'll get good grades, make money, find the perfect spouse, and achieve happiness without major problems because Jesus is on your side. Translated: you want the same things everybody else does? Be a Christian and God will be on your team so you can have them. Then come the normal problems of growing up, and our youth learn that girlfriends break up with them, they don't get the first job they wanted (at the video rental store most likely!), and their grades drop as they chase immediate pleasures.

These ideas of happiness are not even shadows of the true joys of being a Christian, where we live for Christ, not for ourselves. It is almost as though we try to convince our children that God will help them have the things their flesh lusts after. Compare the list of things most teens think will make them happy to the fruit of the Spirit we'll be examining. Pretty different, aren't they? I believe this explains the second reason our children leave the faith.

Bisset's third reason kids leave the faith is that other things become more important to them. The story of Alice illustrates this well. Friends and fun became more important to her than the faith. This is often true of teens, and Alice is to be commended for at least being forthright about it. Her complacent view of the faith says she has come to believe it's easy enough to accept Christ when it's convenient, and that might be after 'enjoying' being young. Peers are notorious for influencing our children, and they tell them listening to the latest music, playing the edgiest video game, wearing the sexiest new styles, and trying the most recent fad are what will make them 'cool', part of the group, and thus happy. Though most teens deny being influenced by peer pressure when directly asked, it is there nonetheless. Part of this is understandable. Adolescents want to find a sense of identity and relatedness that is in some degree independent of their parents. This is a strong drive, yet one that genuinely embracing Christ fulfills.

One place we adults contribute to this mindset is with respect to money. I regrettably am convinced that most children of Christian parents are taught that the primary reason to work hard in school is to get into a good college so you can make a lot of money, implicitly communicating that this is the road to happiness. Yet, when our children become overtly materialistic, we seem surprised. More than we want to think, our lifestyles speak loudly that this is our motivation, too.

Bisset's last reason for why our children leave the faith is that they never owned it for themselves. When they are little, you can make them go to church and sit through family worship.

As they age, they may simply not embrace the faith as their own, and thus refuse to participate in worship. The doctrine of the covenant gives us reason to hope that our children will come to faith, yet somehow they sometimes do not do so. How might this be? Many reasons might be given, but part of it may be that we do a better job of punishing bad behavior than of praying for our children and taking deliberate steps to give them opportunity to learn God's faithfulness for themselves. Christian child-raising must teach the gospel and obedience to Christ, not just focus on correcting bad behaviors. The sinfulness of the human heart means God's grace is necessary.

Our secular and hedonistic culture poses grave dangers to us and to our children. Yet, we must first accept that we as parents and Christian leaders have great room to improve the ways we train our children into the faith of our Lord Jesus Christ. We must provide a firm foundation to equip our children to stand against the culture. This shortcoming contributes to the problem of prodigals, yet demonstrates the vital need for training children into a love for the things of God over the things of the world, and to a desire for the Spirit's fruit in their lives.

The Works of the Flesh

So, whether or not it is directly due to failure of parents, we know many of our children and youth display more works of the flesh than fruits of the Spirit. It is therefore essential that we look at the less popular list of Galatians 5 to better understand this problem, and to point us in directions that may help children in changing.

Hendriksen[7] reminds us that freedom in Christ is a major theme of Galatians, one revisited by Paul in chapter 5 partly because the Judaizers feared Paul's message of salvation through Christ apart from the law would lead to lawlessness, and partly because the Galatian believers still struggled with some of their pagan vices. The latter, of course, leads to his discussion of the works of the flesh, a list which may summarize many of the tribulations encountered by our prodigal children in our increasingly pagan culture.

Hendriksen sees Paul combating the notion that liberty is 'the right to sin' and freedom as 'the privilege to do whatever one's evil heart *wants to* do' (p. 210, emphasis his). How much this sounds like the thinking of contemporary young people! Many children and teens hear in the media and from friends that they should be free to do as this wish, apart from the constraints of rules. Hendriksen sees modern adults at fault as well, defending worldly amusements and other baneful practices as part of our Christian liberty. It may not take much of this manner of thought to get children headed on a path away from God rather than to him, as 'a little leaven leavens the whole lump' (Gal. 5: 10). Rather, what separates the believer from others is the freedom to follow Christ, not the freedom to indulge the flesh. Our freedom permits us through love to serve one another (v. 13), thereby fulfilling the whole law. One wonders how often our words, let alone our lives, send this message to our children. In this we are free to serve others. This is contrasted with what might basically be called selfishness.

As a psychologist, I fear I must admit that my profession has done more to promote selfishness than just about any other. Christian parents often believe instilling 'self-esteem' in their children is the highest goal for their children, and buy the world's philosophy that this is accomplished by giving children everything they want, praising them always, and rarely correcting them. Our church youth programs often appeal to such philosophies in designing programs to attract youth. Yet, such selfishness stands in contrast to the virtues of our faith, and indeed leads directly to the vices detailed in verses 19–21.

The list of fleshly works here largely parallels other such lists, such as 2 Corinthians 12: 20–21. There are 15 items in our present list, though some items overlap.

The first three are sexual sins, the terms being broad enough to encompass the thoughts and desires of the heart. The third term, translated 'sensuality' in the ESV, emphasizes the lack of self-control of the person who gives free reign to his sinful nature. How accurately this describes the sexual behavior of many of today's young people! Sexual stimulation is as near as the television set, the Internet, the lyrics of popular music, or simply looking at the skimpy or sagging clothing of the other kids at school. This area is a downfall in many Christian homes, for parents as well as children. Parents may allow children to dress immodestly, tolerate sexuality on television, or even join in sexual jesting in an effort to be as 'cool' to our kids.

The next two works of the flesh refer to false gods. John Calvin, of course, described our hearts as 'idol factories', though today we miss this point by glibly saying we love God above all, avoiding self-reflection and searching by the Spirit (Ps. 139: 23–4). Many times our behavior betrays the truth, that we love self more than God, and substituting self for God is the heart of idolatry.

It is a bit surprising that the next eight items, over half of the list, relate to strife with others. Of course, this related to particular problems in the Galatian churches, yet relational problems are rife in our day. Many of the mass murders at American schools in recent years have been fueled by the anger of students toward those who rejected and ridiculed them. How much enmity our children see in the lives of parents, those at their churches, and among their peers! Yet this is of the flesh, driven by loving self more than loving God and others. Remember, 'love does not envy or boast; it is not arrogant or rude. It does not insist on its own way; it is not irritable or resentful' (1 Cor. 13: 4b). Christian parents can easily overlook problems in the relationships of (and with) their children because they are so alert to the 'bigger' problems of rebellion, alcohol, or sex.

Not that these aren't on this list, for drunkenness appears in verse 21. 'Orgies', as the ESV translates the Greek, refer to debauched pagan revelries. The contemporary versions of these are the parties thrown in homes when parents are out, or in fraternity houses on college campuses. This is seen in the new teen trend of 'hooking up' where fun is the only incentive for sexual encounters, romance or commitment being passé. The media readily oblige the curious by bringing debauchery into our homes via movies, television, and music lyrics.

The works of the flesh are lamentably easy to find in our churches, homes, and even our children. The root of them is placing self in the place of God, and seeking freedom to sin rather than freedom from sin and to serve.

How do we change our lives, and the lives of our prodigal children? The key, according to Paul, is to build virtue, not just eliminate vice. 'Walk by the Spirit, and you will not gratify the desires of the flesh' (v. 16), or, as Hendriksen reflects, 'It is only the good that can push out the bad' (p. 214).

This exposes a common error we make with our children, prodigal or not. We are quick to dole out punishments when our children err, but slow to teach them the positive truths of Scripture and to guide them into a daily walk with God. We won't just force out the works of the flesh; they must be supplanted by the Spirit and his fruit. We find it easier to punish and think our efforts will succeed than to concede that the battle is spiritual and requires faith and dependence on God.

Galatians 5: 17–18 suggests there is a raging battle between the Spirit and the flesh. This battle is a positive sign of spiritual life in our children, for if the Spirit is not present, the flesh will have its way. The most troubling sign in our prodigals is a lack of conflict in their souls, when they simply don't care that they are sinning. One wonders if such young people are in the Kingdom of God, and our prayers should follow that implication.

I am grateful that, in my experience, most children from Christian homes who are prodigals in some way feel the clash in their souls between the leading of the Spirit and the power of the flesh. Here is cause for hope, for where the Spirit of God is, there is power to move our children toward his fruit and away from the works of the flesh. In our final section for this chapter, I will make some suggestions for parents whose children appear to be losing this battle.

Following Through

For all children, there is no underestimating the power of prayer, yet how vital this is for the lives of prodigals! Don't be embarrassed, but seek out the support and prayers of others. If parents in your church were honest, you'd quickly learn that others struggle as you do. Make the spiritual well-being of your children a regular topic in prayers at your church. For example, our church has a parent prayer meeting during the time the youth group meets. Teach children the Bible faithfully and lovingly. They need to see that you love God's Word and find

31

joy in following Christ. This is far more convincing than using the Bible only as a tool for correcting them. Here are some suggestions by age group.

PRESCHOOLERS

Preschoolers, of course, are not in a position to be as 'prodigal' as older children, yet they can be exhausting in their energy and even defiance. Here are a few ideas for parents of these little ones:

See that they get enough rest. Most parents underestimate how much sleep children of all ages need, and sleep deprivation leads to irritability, and thus increases bad behavior.

Use Bible stories and other morally positive stories to develop a sense of right and wrong.

Use discipline that is firm, but calm. Small children who tantrum often feed off the anger of parents and escalate. Your firm, calm demeanor can help these small ones regain composure. Still give consequences, but don't match yelling with yelling.

Teach them early that they will not get every thing they want. Feel free to say no, and mean it. Never, ever, ever give in once you've said no. This teaches them to manipulate and bargain, and they can be quite skilled at these!

SCHOOL-AGED CHILDREN

Even before they reach double-digits in age, children can become obstinate and mean. Don't wait for them to outgrow it, take action. Consider the following:

Take care to rule out any possible physical explanations for bad moods, such as sleep loss, allergies, learning problems, or poor nutrition (a serious problem in this fast food era).

Use consistent and fair discipline. Punish bad behavior, but also praise and reward them for being good.

Teach them empathy. Use stories and media programs as opportunities to discuss how others feel when children act in certain ways. The Golden Rule of doing unto others as you would have them do to you is still a wonderful guide! This requires the child to set aside selfishness to consider the perspective of others.

Involve your children in helping others. Visit older people, take a meal to someone who is sick, make gifts for the poor, serve at a homeless shelter, tutor disadvantaged children. One of the greatest shortcomings in Christian homes today is the failure to involve children in these types of ministries. We complain because they are selfish, but don't teach them to share and care for others.

Choose their social contexts wisely. Peers are undoubtedly growing influences during these years, and bad behavior and negative attitudes are contagious, caught from mischievous peers. Especially at this age, you have great control over which children your kids spend time with. This includes carefully choosing schools, sports teams, clubs, and such for your children.

Prayerfully consider seeking counsel. This might be a pastor, children's minister, a mature saint, or even a professional Christian counselor. Proverbs makes clear that wise people seek counsel, and we need great wisdom to raise children in this demanding age!

ADOLESCENTS

This is the age when most prodigals surface. Great patience is needed, and those who care for the prodigals must never slack in prayer and hope. Remember Monica, the mother of the great Saint Augustine who prayed for years with great diligence before seeing her prodigal come to faith in Christ.

Keep your head out of the sand. Don't be naïve about the dangers of modern life. Keep up with the news; know what your sons and daughters are facing out there.

Monitor media closely. We'll be saying more about this, but teens are stealthy in getting to materials that fuel rebellion.

Keep communication flowing. Ask specific questions, like 'Who did you sit with at lunch today?' rather than general ones like 'How was your day?'

Monitor their whereabouts. This may be the single best way to keep young people out of trouble.

Show them your love despite their faults; don't let your anger and frustration overwhelm you so that is all they see.

Make difficult decisions. Not doing anything is a passive decision to leave the situation unchanged. Terminate bad friendships, change their schools, take the car keys. In general, let them know you are committed to protecting them.

Teach your children to earn freedoms by demonstrating responsibilities. If you want to do such and such (e.g., go shopping by yourself), you can show me by faithfully doing this thing (e.g., remembering to do your chores). Privileges come because they are earned, not because your teen persuades you.

Despite the problems you are having, still try to encourage the Spirit's fruit in their lives. Keep reading this book prayerfully and hopefully.

As stated above, do not be hesitant to seek counsel from a godly person or even a professional Christian counselor.

3

WHY FOCUS ON THE FRUIT?

Life is hectic these days. It's rare to meet someone who doesn't feel 'stressed' by the busyness of life. Jobs demand more hours. Often both parents work to make ends meet, rushing home to fix dinner for the children, or grabbing fast food *en route*. Kids, too, seem busier. Schools increase expectations for homework, sports teams demand more time, and clubs and organizations are more like part-time jobs given the time demands they place on our children. We struggle to keep our heads above water amid all this craziness. We think we are busy doing good things, but this often has a subtle yet profound impact on our parenting.

This lifestyle lends itself to what I call 'reactive parenting', a tendency to let children be unless they do something bad or seriously inconvenience a parent. This means bad behavior is likely to meet with punishment, though not consistently as the parent may at times be too preoccupied to address the offence. This also means children may receive little parental attention by being good, making misbehavior more attractive. To quote a former colleague's phrase that captures children's thinking, 'Love me, hate me, but don't ignore me.'

Most often such parenting focuses on surviving the stress of life. The day has too much in it already to spare time for children's problems, so they are met with little patience. Often such parenting is done in stress-filled anger, the parent reacting excessively to the provocation by the child. This may lead to the parent feeling guilt and a sense of needing to make it up to the child, thus beginning a pattern of erratic angry explosions followed by permissiveness. When we stop to look at this, no one sees this as healthy or biblical. Nonetheless, the reactive parenting style captures the predominant theme in parenting today: giving consequences for misbehavior.

We rush to point out transgressions. We'll correct our son's bad language, or ground our teen when she comes in too late. We don't let our children watch 'dirty' movies or listen to music with crude lyrics. We punish lying and disrespectful actions. You might say we are like police, enforcing rules but not teaching proper thinking and behavior. We major in 'don'ts' and are weak on the 'do's'. Most books on child-rearing focus primarily on how to discipline them for misbehavior. Many parents I speak with believe their problems with their children lie in their poor techniques of disciplining misbehavior, and are eager for better disciplinary strategies.

While there are several criticisms we might level at such an approach, the most important may be that it fails to teach the next generation a Christian understanding of life and the world. It gives the impression that being a Christian means not doing certain 'bad' things while otherwise enjoying the same things as everyone else, at least up to a point. It does not communicate the higher joy we find in Christ, and living for him. Nor does it call children away from self-interest to the pursuit of holiness. It does not ask us to be different from the world.

Philip Gourevitch[1] graphically portrays how the West stood idly by as some 800,000 people were slaughtered during the genocide in Rwanda in 1994. Western nations had denounced the Nazi extermination of Jews and vowed never to let this happen again, but did nothing in Rwanda as it largely had in similar situations since the 1940's. In response, Gourevitch laments, 'denouncing evil is a far cry from doing good.'[2] We denounced the evil, but were passive when we might have done good.

This might also accurately summarize the approach of reactive Christian parents as we face the world of the 21st century. We denounce the bad things to which our children are exposed and even take part in. Yet, we fail to teach them to do the good that should follow directly from following Christ. Or stated even more directly to our theme, such parenting denounces the lust of the flesh without exalting the goal of bearing the Spirit's fruit. Our children learn they shouldn't act badly, but are not taught to love and pursue the Christian virtues. This makes even less sense when we remember, as we noted in the previous chapter, that in Galatians 5: 16 we prevent gratification of the lusts of the flesh not by will power or severe punishments, but by walking in the Spirit. As Hendriksen states it, 'Vice can only be conquered by virtue.'[3]

Research on parenting bears out this point. Diana Baumrind[4] found that the basic styles of parenting vary along two dimensions: control and nurture. Parents who are low in controlling and nurturing their children are deemed neglectful, with their children growing to show little self-control and to have poor social skills. Parents who nurture but exert little authority over their children are indulgent. This sadly reflects many Christian parents who have believed the cultural insistence on providing for children's every whim, while being lax in discipline and demanding very little of their children. The result? Children who can't control their behavior yet always expect to have their way. The third pattern is also common among Christians, particularly among conservative ones. These are parents (most often fathers, I must concede) who are highly controlling but weak in nurture toward their sons and daughters. This 'authoritarian' style may yield children who are anxious, passive, and have poor communication skills. Here we see the result of stressing consequences of misbehavior without the concomitant encouragement of positive virtues. The most successful parents, per Baumrind, are high in control and nurture. This authoritative style is most likely to produce socially-responsible young people who are better able to take care of themselves. This reinforces the importance of controlling the behavior of children, yet suggests that nurturing and cultivating the positive virtues are essential to produce good kids. How much more true is this for Christians

37

who model the love of God to their children and teach them to be virtuous in the biblical sense. Why, then, are we struggling to properly parent our children?

Freedom to Serve God, Not Ourselves

I grimace as I must once again acknowledge that my profession, psychology, may be a major contributor to this failure. Psychology has stressed the virtues of self: self-esteem, self-worth, self-service, self-efficacy, self-fulfillment, self-reliance, and self-direction. What a paradox that parents have often sacrificed themselves to promote the self-centeredness of their children, trading their Christian birthrights for a mess of psychological porridge! Even a secular psychologist such as Jean Twenge, in her recent book *Generation Me: Why Today's Young Americans Are More Confident, Assertive, Entitled—and More Miserable Than Ever Before* finds that the self-focus of parents has led to narcissistic and unhappy children.

As believers, we send a contradictory message to our children by speaking out against the excesses of self-indulgence without striking at the root of self-centeredness. Our children consequently believe that Christian life consists of having as good a time as possible so long as you don't hurt anyone or get too carried away. In fact, Jesus is on our team to see to it that we have the nicest things, the best health, the best education, the best social circles, the best relationships, and the most fun… the good, clean type, of course. We are free in Christ, and so should enjoy the pleasures of the world he has given us.

I am not denying that God wants us to enjoy his world, and I am not saying that enjoying ourselves appropriately is bad. What I am saying is this pursuit of earthly pleasure is not what being Christian is about. It is not about merely denouncing evil; rather, it is about doing and being good. Strangely enough, it is in doing good that our children will find the greatest happiness. Even secular psychologists such as Martin Seligman[5] are beginning to see this light, though they miss the larger picture of God's glory. Seligman had his students complete two projects, one being to indulge themselves in a favorite activity, and the other being to perform an act of kindness. When the results were compared, he learned the students felt happier performing the act of kindness than the one of self-indulgence.

This has been the message of a tradition of Christian writers such as John Piper who argues that we are made for joy, but the joy is of the Lord and we find it in pursuing him.[6] Christians have a deeper understanding of what genuine pleasure is. A child might consider candy to be delicious, but an adult has different tastes, and may reserve the term 'delicious' for steak or seafood. One's taste betrays one's nature. So it is with our pleasures. When we focus our lives on God, we will demonstrate the good of the Spirit's fruit and find great pleasure in so doing. Our joys are now rooted in pleasing God, and as we desire to bear spiritual fruit in pursuit of God's pleasure, that in turn brings us profound pleasure.

Let me illustrate this point with the biblical phrase 'the beauty of holiness' found in passages such as Psalm 29: 2 and 96: 9 (note that the ESV translates the phrase as 'the splendor of holiness'). Just as with taste, one's appreciation of beauty also tells something about the person. A teenager may think a pop love ballad is 'beautiful' music while a parent might see it as silly, considering a work like Handel's *Messiah* to exemplify true beauty. We might call it a more mature perception of the nature of beauty.

The genuine Christian, then, has a new 'taste' and sees splendor or beauty in the holiness of God. Here indeed is a marvelous transformation! In our sinful nature, we are inclined to hide from holiness and find beauty in the pleasures of the flesh. It takes no spiritual maturity to find delight in the things most people do: a nice house, fine car, financial success, lots of friends, a 'good time' at the movies or a concert, sexual intimacy, a meal at a favorite restaurant, or even a quiet evening reading by a fireplace. It is not that these pleasures are inherently bad. By no means! All of these can be beautiful in their way. Yet, for the Christian, these fade before the beauty of a holy God. We find beauty in the Giver more than in his gifts. We exult in God's nature more than his benefits to us.

Though once we were sinners and loved our sin, we now can see that God's holiness is beautiful, not terrifying. The genuine Christian life is marked by a God-given joy in his holiness and the desire to imitate it in one's life. The true believer has different aspirations, goals, and values when compared to the unbelievers around her, and so we desire to see these in the lives of our children as well. Time outs and spankings don't produce this difference in our offspring. They, too, must forsake the desires of the flesh and grow in the love of God and his holiness.

From where does such a desire come? As parents, what do we do with our children to promote this change of 'taste'? Galatians 5 gives the answer in verse 13: Christians are called to freedom. At first glance, this sounds like an affirmation of the very problem we are confronting. Kids want freedom quite naturally. But the freedom children seek naturally is freedom for self, to do what they want to do. Your typical teen is not complaining that his parents' rules keep him from studying the Bible as he wants. Rather, he pines about rules keeping him from staying out late with his friends, from seeing questionable movies, or from listening to the music he craves.

Now, look again at our text. Christian freedom is not to gratify the flesh, but to serve one another (and thus God) in love. This captures quite well the problem we've been discussing. We must not give our children the impression that life is about serving self and the Bible just shows us how to do it in a 'righteous' way so you can do it without getting in trouble. Rather, we must communicate that being a Christian frees us from blindly following the lusts of the flesh and frees us to find beauty in serving others. Freedom is not the liberty to indulge ourselves, but liberation from the flesh so we may serve others. The fruit of the Spirit, then, is the grace needed for this service to others, which in turn brings us true spiritual joy.

Verse 14 completes the thought, showing that such love of neighbor fulfills the law, implying that we are not seeking our own or given to our own pleasures. Calvin pinpoints the problem of self-love: 'If men were not so given to self-love as they be, there would be good love and agreement among all men.'[7] Rather, 'the honor that we must yield to God, is to renounce ourselves, to the end we may love them that hate us.'[8] Such love, not legalistic prohibitions, fulfills the Great Commandment to love God and neighbor with all our being

(Deut. 6: 5; Lev. 19: 18; Matt. 19: 19; 22: 37; Mark 12: 30–31; Luke 10: 27).

Why, then, focus on the fruit of the Spirit? To see this fruit manifest in the lives of our children indicates they have indeed renounced themselves and found the freedom to serve God and others, therein knowing truly Christian happiness and pursuit of the truly beautiful. This is a dramatically different approach to life than they will find in the media and the culture, and implies our children will be trained to look far beyond the things of the world for their lasting joy. As Christian parents, we must teach, model, pray for, and promote a life of self-denial to free our children to fulfill the original calling of persons, to glorify God and to enjoy him forever.

The Battle Begins!

The disquieting implication of this is that Christian parents will not aspire to raise 'successful' children in the eyes of the world, but to train soldiers who will do battle against the world, the flesh, and the devil. 'The desires of the flesh are against the Spirit, and the desires of the Spirit are against the flesh, for these are opposed to each other, to keep you from doing the things you want to do' (Gal. 5: 17). 'We do not wrestle against flesh and blood, but against the cosmic powers over this present darkness, against the spiritual forces of evil in the heavenly places' (Eph. 6: 12). We easily miss the realm of the true battle. We teach our children to be competitive in school, knowing that good grades lead to good jobs. We coach our children to be intense combatants on the sports field, knowing that grit and determination will win the game. But do we overlook the most important battleground, found in the spiritual lives of our children?

Paul's contrast of the works of the flesh with the fruit of the Spirit exposes the stakes of the battle, and these could not be higher. In so doing, his words hark back to when Jesus called his disciples away from pursuit of worldly goals and to discipleship by calling them to deny themselves, take up their cross, and follow him. 'For what will it profit a man if he gains the whole world and forfeits his life?' (Matt. 16: 26a). Our children will not ultimately profit from educational, economic, or social success, but from victory in the spiritual battle of, and for, their lives. Do the children under your charge know they are not only preparing for battle, but are in one already? We cannot give our children the impression that being Christians makes life easier or that God exists merely to help us reach earthly goals. Rather, we must, by God's grace, communicate to our children that a battle for their souls is raging, one that pits the lusts of their flesh against the self-denial and love of others that God requires. The battle cannot be fought by human means. It must be fought by active pursuit of God's power in the Holy Spirit and a passionate longing for his fruit in their lives.

The world, the flesh, and the devil conspire to undermine the spiritual lives of your children. They would claim them as the spoil of battle. As their guardians, we cannot be oblivious to this. We cannot be complacent. The battlefield is no place for 'taking it easy' or 'going with the flow'. We must not let our children fraternize with the enemy, or be seduced by his wiles. We are compelled to be on high alert through prayer and an intimate walk with our Lord, and to forewarn our children of the dangers around them. We are to train them to resist the world, but also to pursue the virtues of their Lord, for the Spirit must win the battle, and his fruit will show us he has.

Calvin stresses that our sinful nature is inclined to inhibit our spiritual progress so 'men must enforce and constrain themselves, and maintain battle as against a deadly enemy, when they intend to go forward in goodness.'[9] The sinful nature we, and our children, must combat includes our thoughts, emotional inclinations, and desires. They do not need mere management, but replacement with the mind and desires of Christ. Simply punishing sin in our children's lives won't do it. Calvin again wisely explains, 'Given the sin which we battle, we must always have our eyes cast heavenward for our everlasting rest.'[10] Thoroughly Christian parenting, then, intends to teach children that their happiness is in their Heavenly Father, something to be fully realized in eternity, and that their lives are to be spent in pursuit of that goal. Orienting lives toward God inevitably intensifies the warfare we have described, pitting our new nature in Christ against the inclinations of sin. This is the true character of the Christian life.

Fruit Conquers Flesh

We now see that the biblical mandate to us as parents is more than just punishing bad behavior. Ours is a more comprehensive task, requiring us to raise our children in the 'discipline and instruction of the Lord' (Eph. 6: 4b). This points us to the proactive commands of Scripture. We teach our children not only not to kill, steal, or covet, but positively to love others, even their enemies. The positive virtue of love is variously broken down into specific virtues in several places in Scripture. The Beatitudes of Matthew 5 are an example of this, extolling the virtues of poverty of spirit, mourning, meekness, longing for righteousness, mercy, purity of heart, peacemaking, and suffering persecution for the sake of Christ's Name. The remainder of Jesus' Sermon on the Mount (Matt. 5–7) develops this even vision of 'true love' even further.

I have chosen the fruit of the Spirit, however, for our discussion. The breadth of the meaning of these wonderful fruit is one reason. Their contrast with the works of the flesh is another, especially as we have seen that the positive virtues overcome the vices. True love and joy prevail over sexual sins and idolatry (loving something more than God) listed in Galatians 5. Patience, kindness, goodness, faithfulness, and gentleness rout the interpersonal sins of enmity, strife, jealousy, anger, rivalries, dissensions, divisions, and envy. The fruit of self-control obliterates the excesses of drunkenness and orgies.

Given that the world, flesh, and devil conspire to draw our children into these vices, it is important to understand how they try to do so, and to see that keeping our children from the grip of these sins is accomplished by the infusion of the Spirit's fruit into their lives. Just as an apple tree by its nature will bear apples as fruit, so the spiritual person by nature will bear such spiritual fruit, as fruit can be defined as 'that which is produced by the inherent energy of a living organism.'[11]

It is therefore essential to stress that parents cannot directly produce the fruit of the Spirit in the lives of their sons and daughters. It is, after all, the Holy Spirit's fruit, not ours. There is no formula for the fruit, and one cannot ultimately view some of the fruit as though they stand independently of the others. The fruit as a group holds together as the outward manifestation of the Christlike character worked in the child's life by the Holy Spirit. The converse can be said of the works of the flesh. These are rarely found in isolation, but huddle together. This is somewhat like the pattern of peer relations in a group of teenagers: the achieving, well-behaved children tend to associate with one another while the more mischievous youth run in the same social circles. Though we will examine these one at a time, let us bear in mind that the group will manifest themselves together in our lives, and the lives of our children. Let us also be mindful that these are ultimately the work of the third Person of the Trinity, and not something we directly produce or control. Our task is to orient our children properly toward Christ and to make them mindful of the contemporary dangers to the faith that might threaten that orientation.

As we consider the list of fruit given by Paul in Galatians 5, we will not assume that the list is comprehensive, just as the roll of fleshly works is not comprehensive. Each child will show fruit in a unique social and cultural context and in harmony with one's particular spiritual giftedness. Holiness is not a formula. We intend merely to consider some of the threads woven into this divine fabric.

Finally, each of us, as persons who care for children and particularly the young ones entrusted to us as parents or Christian workers, knows that we must model in our lives what we would teach to our children. To ask of our children what we do not demonstrate in our lives is to be guilty of hypocrisy, and children often spot this more quickly than adults. Though the chapters to follow will speak particularly of the threats our children face, and consider ways to help their walks with Christ, each of us must also examine ourselves. As we walk more faithfully by the Spirit, and display his fruit more fully in our lives, it will be easier and even more natural for our children to follow.

A pastor friend of mine illustrates being filled with the Spirit with an image of sailboats. The wind would blow over the water, but to catch the breeze, the sails had to be completely unfurled. Once fully extended, the sails would fill with the breeze, which then would carry the boat along with it. The Holy Spirit, like the wind to which he is often compared, is blowing in our day. We want to unfurl our sails to be moved along with him, and to keep our children's sails from being tangled with the cares of the world and free to yield to the Spirit's movement so as to manifest his fruit in their lives. Here is the hope of Christian parents, the hope we intend to pursue in the chapters that follow as we closely consider each of the Spirit's fruit and ways the world would entangle our children in them. By so doing, I pray we will be God's instrument in keeping his children unstained by the world.

4

LOVE AND ITS IMITATIONS

It captured the attention of all the world's children, the greatest contest in history. Who would find the five gold tickets hidden in Wonka chocolate bars? The eccentric recluse Willie Wonka would host the lucky winners and allow them to see the marvels of his magnificent chocolate factory.

Selfish desire brings out the worst in people, and four of the five winners were children who proved to be selfish in varied but typical ways. Veruca Salt is the consummate spoiled rich kid, whining until her parents concede to her every whim. Mike Teavee is gifted with an analytical mind, and all too proud of the fact. Living in a world of video games and irritated by anyone who might distract him, he got his ticket by figuring out how to beat the system. Authority would never rule over this thirteen-year-old.

Violet Beauregarde inherited her mother's competitiveness, amassing 263 trophies and medals in her brief ten years. Every activity of life is an opportunity to prove herself better than others. She even takes her gum chewing very seriously, chewing the same piece for weeks to break a record. No other child will stand in her way of getting the recognition she covets. Augustus Gloop is a German boy who lives to eat candy, greedily consuming it in extraordinary excess as his parents passively fuel his appetite lest they stifle their son's desires. He is a living example of gluttony, pursuing happiness in a nonstop sugar high, oblivious to the effect on his parents' wallet or his pants size.

We will find many opportunities in our study to criticize the movies of our day and the movie-watching habits of our children. But in fairness, we consider the 2004 Willie Wonka remake, *Charlie and the Chocolate Factory*, as an exception in that it exposes and criticizes the self-absorption of today's children. Each of the children above met an unpleasant fate because of their self-centeredness. Only our hero, Charlie Bucket, is admirable. Despite coming from a poor home, he loves, and his family love him. Charlie even chooses a life of poverty with his family over riches apart from them. Charlie comes closer to reflecting the biblical notion of love than do his self-obsessed competitors for the grand prize (which, of course, Charlie wins).

The selfish children in this story cleverly stereotype the products of modern Western culture and parenting, even among Christian families. Trained by experts, media, and most of all by advertisers, parents strive to guarantee that their children have self-esteem above all. And, they are told, such self-esteem will make their children happy and successful. Such indulgent parenting may make children superficially self-confident, but also makes them so at the expense of learning to love and respect others.

When arrogant Veruca meets her fate in vain pursuit of yet something else she feels entitled to have (a highly skilled squirrel), the accompanying musical number in the movie knows where to point the finger.

> Who went and spoiled her, who indeed?
> Who pandered to her every need?
> Who turned her into such a brat?
> Who are the culprits, who did that?
> The guilty ones, now this is sad.
> Are dear old mum, and loving dad.

It is indeed sad that parents today are awash in the philosophy and culture of the age. This is even more lamentable in that these parents are mostly well-meaning, trying to do what they understand to be right. Yet, they still manage to raise children who are consumed with themselves.

In contrast to such self-absorption, Christian character is marked by love above all. This is not love of self, but love of God, others, and our neighbor. As we noted in the previous chapter, the Great Commandment sums up God's commands to love God with all your being, and your neighbor as yourself (Matt. 22: 37–9). The scriptural mandate goes even further, insisting that we love even our enemies (Matt. 5: 44). If I may say so rather straighforwardtly, focusing directly on building our children's self-esteem by always praising and indulging them will never lead to their displaying the Spirit's fruit of love.

I figure that most of us already know that. It's just that the world around us presses its message so aggressively that we lose sight of this. We want children who have Charlie's character, not the egoism of the other four children in the story. To that end, let us consider the nature of biblical love, how it is threatened in our time, and what we can do to promote our children developing into loving followers of Christ.

Biblical Love

Love is an extensive theme in the Bible, and space does not allow us to mine all its riches. We will limit our discussion to three primary topics: Love to God and neighbor, the Love Chapter (1 Cor. 13), and the outworking of Christian love.

LOVE TO GOD AND NEIGHBOR

The Great Commandment is a powerful call to love in a manner encompassing all of the Law and the Prophets, according to Jesus in Matthew 22: 40. Love to God is the first aspect of this summary statement. God is himself love (1 John 4: 8), and this is why the Christlike believer is to echo that love. 'We love because he first loved us,' says John (1 John 4: 19). How do we recognize God's love? Not in any form of selfishness, but in his great love for fallen mankind (John 3: 16) and his willingness to sacrifice his only begotten Son for our salvation. The Second Person of the Trinity responds in kind by self-denying obedience, becoming flesh and blood out of love for the Father and for his wayward human 'sheep'. To receive the benefits of such love and not respond in kind is the height of ingratitude. We cannot let our children be ungrateful for God's love, and teaching thankfulness is a central part of Christian parenting. This begins with things as basic as insuring that a child says 'thank you' when someone gives her a gift or compliment. As we know, children learn more by seeing than by being told, so it is fundamental that parents and Christian adults around our children demonstrate loving gratitude in our lives.

Love to God flows from our abiding in relationship with the Father (1 John 4: 16), for those alienated from God fear him rather than love him. Christian love is cultivated only in the hearts of believers, and in the context of our daily fellowship with God. Søren Kierkegaard beautifully explains, 'As the quiet lake is fed deep down by the flow of hidden springs, which no eye sees, so a human being's love is grounded, still more deeply, in God's love.'[1] Our children again must witness this process in our lives and be directed to the hidden springs of God's love. It will not be enough simply to tell our children to love God; this must be modeled, prayed for, and encouraged. We must ask ourselves if our daily priorities and ways of talking support or betray our professed love for God.

John goes further to challenge our profession of love to God by saying, 'If anyone says, 'I love God,' and hates his brother, he is a liar; for he who does not love his brother whom he has seen cannot love God whom he has not seen' (1 John 4: 20). He proceeds to tie this directly to the Great Commandment in verse 21, 'And this commandment we have from him: whoever loves God must also love his brother.' In a nutshell, if we do not love others around us, we fool ourselves if we believe we love God. These two commandments are inextricably woven together.

Loving our neighbor is where we can, in a sense, see more of genuine love than in our relationship with God. God is always worthy of love, and his benefits to us are measureless. Once we are redeemed, it is merely natural to love the One who has done and continues to do so much for us. But loving other people is a different story. People have sinful natures, and are not always loveable. They let us down. They don't give us what we want. They may not respond to our acts of kindness in the way we wish. They even hurt us intentionally at times. Here the true nature of love is revealed: it must be directed to the good of the other and not of the self, regardless of any benefit to self in so doing. This is the heart of agape, though it is alien to the world around us. Romans 5: 8 teaches us that God showed his love to us by dying for us while we were still sinners. He did not respond to any gestures of affection on our part. No, he reached out to us while we were still rebels, giving his life to transform us even when we did not want to change. This is authentic love.

The gap between how loveable we may be and how loveable our neighbor may be is infinitesimal compared to the gap God spanned to save us in our sinfulness. Therefore, in relation to God's love, our love for our faulty, frail, human neighbor is a small thing to ask. When we fail to love our neighbor, we realize that we have yet to grasp God's love for us. This is a call for us to pray for ourselves and our children as Paul prayed for the Ephesians, imploring God that they 'may have strength to comprehend with all the saints what is the breadth and length and height and depth, and to know the love of Christ that surpasses all knowledge, that you may be filled with all the fullness of God' (3: 18–19).

Consider that such love is determined by love itself, not by the attractiveness of its object. Kierkegaard again is helpful: 'Erotic love is determined by the object; friendship is determined by the object; only love to one's neighbour is determined by love.'[2] Kierkegaard (among others) maintains that 'neighbor' refers to anyone, so we are not to look for loveliness in the recipient of neighbor love, but to consider everyone the same. Love for love's sake is selfless, not bound up in the attractiveness of the object to our senses and wants. This is well illustrated by parents who give birth to a deformed child, yet love him dearly nonetheless.

How much are we to love our neighbor? As much as we love ourselves. Observe several important points here. First, the text does not say we must learn to love ourselves before we can love our neighbor. Jesus assumes we love ourselves. This seems to be almost universally true. One can argue that even suicide is an act of self-love, with the person choosing to hurt those around him in order to escape his personal pain.

Suicide is most often built on the belief that death will reduce suffering and so a person may choose death as the least painful alternative, the best option available for self.

But also note that Jesus does not tell us not to love ourselves. Such love of self seems reasonable and even necessary. We feed ourselves, see to it that we are rested, comfortable, safe, and happy, and we work hard to achieve these things. Yet such self-love is intended by God only as a means to a greater end, not an end in itself. We are to care for ourselves so we are fit for the spiritual battle of life. For soldiers to eat and rest before the battle is not indulgent, but part of being a good soldier. However, if the soldier is so focused on comfort and food that he forgets the battle and pursues only his comfort, he is a poor soldier indeed. So it is with the Christian soldier: self-love enables other-love. The former is natural; the latter is a work of God's Spirit in the believer's life.

Love for neighbor is to be measured against love for self. How eagerly we provide for our own wants and wishes, seeing that we are free from pain and suffering as best we can! We feel hurt if someone speaks ill of us. We take care to see that we are safe, and we see that needs (and many wants) are met. Neighbor love says that we care for the comfort and well-being of all those around us in the same way. This is a high and challenging calling indeed! We must move past the Darwinian concept that we are competing with others for survival, and live biblically as did our Lord, humbly counting others to be more significant than ourselves (Phil. 2: 3).

Even in writing this, I am convicted. Where can our children see such love demonstrated? Who may we point to and tell our children, 'Love as she loves'? I fear most of us are poor examples of such love. We spend exorbitant amounts of money to entertain ourselves without a thought for the deadly poverty in developing nations. We spend our time in front of the television set when widows in our churches sit at home literally dying of loneliness. We as Christian adults must learn to love our neighbors, teaching our children to do the same as we do. As a rule, our children need to witness and experience such love before we can expect it to appear in their lives.

LOVE YOUR ENEMIES

The biblical expectations for the Christian are more challenging still. Sometimes our neighbor is our enemy, and we are to love our enemies (Matt. 5: 43–4; Luke 6: 27–8). Here we strike at the heart of God's love. The most remarkable thing about God's greatest gift was that Jesus died for us while we were sinners (Rom. 5: 8). Paul explains further that this meant 'while we were enemies we were reconciled to God by the death of his Son' (Rom. 5: 10). Jesus asks us to do for our enemies nothing more than he did for us. If we are to manifest the love of God, we must love our enemies as well. As we have noted, this is less to ask of us than it was of God, as he in his perfect holiness loved us while we were still rebellious sinners. We, who still struggle with sin, are asked to love enemies who are sinful like us. Only God's forgiving grace makes us different from the greatest sinner in the world, be it the most murderous terrorist, the wealthy financier who exploits the poor, or simply the person in my workplace who threatens my job. Moreover, this was not a theme new to Jesus. It appears in Old Testament passages such as Exodus 23: 4–5 which teaches us to respect the property of our enemies.

Pastor and author John Piper tells us that the early Christian treatment of enemy love 'answers the question, "How shall I treat my enemy?" with the unequivocal and unqualified demand upon the believer not to repay evil with evil but, positively, to do good, bless, pray for, seek peace, in short to love. This love is grounded in the mercies of God experienced by the believer in Christ and it aims ultimately at the enemies' enjoyment of that mercy.'[3]

How does such a powerful mission play in the early twenty-first century? First, our culture would have us think there are no such things as enemies, for we are to tolerate all positions and lifestyles. This idea, however, leads only to indifference and not to love. That is assuming it works as a philosophy in the first place. 'Tolerant' people tend to hate 'intolerant' people who believe in absolute right and wrong. So this view collapses on itself in irrationality.

Most people indeed have enemies of some sort. There are those distant enemies who hate us simply for being Westerners, matched by our tendency to hate people of different cultures or faiths as well. The fallout from the Crusades still haunts us. But even closer to home, we have those neighbors or even church members who we just don't like, or who, for some reason, just don't like us. There are those who resent our success, faith, or relationships.

This trend is more obvious in the youth culture. For all the preaching done about tolerance, violence and hatred persist. Witness the recent mass killings in American schools by disgruntled teens who were constantly teased and ostracized. Gangs wage lethal warfare in many cities. Hatred can also be subtle. The sophisticated bullying among girls, especially during the early teen years, is gaining increased attention.[4] Much could be said about the culture of violence among children spurred on by television, movies, and video games, but we will save this discussion for a bit later. The point here is that our children and we have adequate opportunity to face 'enemies' and thus to demonstrate love for them as commanded by our Lord.

As parents, we need to assess carefully what our children hear us say about others. Do we complain about others, gripe about the Sunday sermon, gossip, or speak cruelly about distant enemies? Or, do our children see and hear us burdened for others, even those whose intentions toward us are not the best? We once again face the sobering fact that we are to model the Christian love that we long to see in our children.

What about our children? First, we must help them to understand more of God's profound love for them as a basis for our love for others, including our enemies. We must help them to find security in their relationship with Christ so that 'enemies' are not so threatening. We should help them see when they are responding to peers in natural, sinful ways, and point them to more godly ways of looking at situations. For example, when a son is angry because he is being teased at school (or, sadly, sometimes even at church!), we express our understanding about how natural that feeling is while gradually guiding him to consider how sad it is that this bully doesn't seem to know the love of God. We wonder with our son whether retribution or being shown mercy might be more effective in convincing the other child of the difference Christ makes in a life. This will take some work, yet this suggests the direction I believe we need to take.

THE LOVE CHAPTER

What survey of major biblical themes about love would be complete without a look at 1 Corinthians 13? In a day where love is often merely the feeling of finding something you like in another person or thing, we need to refresh our memories of the deep, spiritual nature of biblical love. Let us briefly consider the qualities of such love.

First, we see that we should prize love above spiritual experience and noble acts (verses 1–2). Ours is a day when many Christians will forsake biblical principles of worship to find an experience. The statistics I cited in Chapter 2 remind us that our teens are becoming more eclectic, if not simply syncretistic, in their spiritual lives, cutting and pasting what will give them a good feeling or memorable experience. Paul shuffles experience into the background to show that love should have center stage in our lives.

The relatedness and essential unity of the fruit of the Spirit is evident as we examine the next qualities of love presented in our text, as several of these are also listed separately as fruit in Galatians 5. Patience and kindness are characteristic of love because it focuses on the other, not self. We are impatient with those we love when we get angry over their failure to give us what we want in the relationship, unveiling whose interests we truly have in mind. Love does not envy or boast as both of these traits reflect self-focused jealousy or the need to think we are in some way superior to another (recall the example of Violet Beauregarde at the outset of this chapter).

Love is neither arrogant nor rude (vv. 4–5), in contrast to Veruca Salt and Mike Teavee in the Wonka story. Arrogance is clear evidence of selfish motives, and rudeness surely does not seek the best for the other. A study of the life of Jesus will not reveal these qualities. Rather, love focuses on and seeks the well-being of the other.

Watch little children (and bigger ones, too) to see how important and natural it is for them to get their own way.

Friendly get-togethers turn ugly due to debates over which video to watch or which game to play. Yet, Scripture tells us love does not insist on its own way (v. 5). Moreover, it is not irritable or resentful. Irritability is incompatible with patience, and again unveils a person who is seeking something for herself in the other, being annoyed when it is not received. It is easy to resent the student who gets the big award or the team-mate who wins Most Valuable Player as they received something we wanted. Yet the ease is because it is a fleshly desire, not an other-focused love. Recall from Chapter 2 how many of the deeds of the flesh involve conflict with others.

Love rejoices with the truth, not wrongdoing. How many children readily snicker when they see a peer or sibling tricked or teased? Even as parents, we have to stifle back a laugh when we witness a good trick played on someone on television or even in real life. Yet if we love the other, there is nothing funny in their mistreatment. Rather, we find joy in seeing godly kindness manifested.

Love is committed to the other. This means it will bear, believe, hope, and endure all things (v. 7). This is how God loves us, persisting despite our ingratitude and failures. This is true of parents' love for their children (in most cases), and it is the glue that holds marriages together. But when love is defined as mutual convenience, divorce and alienation become options.

Paul stresses (vv. 8–12) that love is never ending. In more theological terms, that means it is eternal. The failures and shortcomings of the object do not excuse withdrawing love. Tongues, knowledge, and prophecy will pass away, but love is eternal. It should continue to grow into eternity as the believer is sanctified, walks more closely with the Lord, and grows in the gift of love as a fruit of the Spirit. Paul's conclusion: love is greater than the other two abiding qualities of faith and hope (v. 13). If this is true, what more important virtue to cultivate in the lives of our children than genuine, other-focused, godly love?

The description of love in this remarkable chapter is intimidating. Consider seeking God's face in prayer to help you choose one of these characteristics that you need to work on in your life, and ask his guidance to take steps to grow in this area while praying for your children in the same manner.

When you see progress on one of these, choose another and continue your family's growth in God's wonderful love.

THE OUTWORKING OF TRUE LOVE

If we love as the Bible teaches, what might it look like in the day-to-day lives of our children? Let me offer a few suggestions while inviting the reader prayerfully to consider how this fruit would look in her own home.

An obvious starting point would be the love between husband and wife. Our children would see in their parents love that focuses on the other, is patient, and seeks and finds peace amid differences. They would see a love that lasts and deepens over time. It is difficult for children to imagine a good marital relationship when they don't see one at home. Beyond this, they should see good examples in the lives of other adults in their church.

Children should also see true Christlike love in the way their parents treat them. They would see generous doses of control and warmth, limit-setting and compassion. Giving in to children by doting on them and letting them do as they please is not a sign of love, and deep down, kids know that. I'll never forget the pubescent boy who told me of an incident with his mother where she did nothing to stop him from playing outside the house with a dangerous weapon. When I looked shocked, he gazed intently at me and said, 'Sometimes you'd think she'd care enough to say "no".' We must love our children deeply enough to teach them right from wrong, even though they might protest at times.

Children should also see love among believers, even as Jesus told his disciples that love would be proof of their discipleship (John 13: 35). The conflict or simple shallowness of many congregations is a major reason children lose love for the church. Recall again how many works of the flesh in Galatians 5 involve problems in relationships. This context even suggests the love mentioned in 5: 22 is primarily love of one's spiritual brothers and sisters in contrast to the bickering seen elsewhere. We must bear in mind that superficial friendliness and niceties are not the same as the love we are discussing.

I believe children should see genuine love in the way we treat our elders. The text for this book, James 1: 27, teaches that one characteristic of pure and undefiled religion is to visit widows in their affliction. Yet, our children often see older family members neglected or disrespected, and the same may be true of older church members. If you do not have an older family member near you that you care for, consider adopting an older person or widow from your church to care for, and involve your children in the project.

Love should be encouraged from child to child. This includes stressing loving one's siblings, with parents actively teaching positive relationships while not tolerating disrespect and rudeness between children in the home. Such love also extends to children's friendships where parents from an early age teach social competence and caring so they can be loving friends.

This background of loving relationships should provide our children with a better concept of true love as they begin to date and move toward marriage. My experience is that many Christian teens have little concept of the nature and depth of true love, and approach romantic relationships viewing love as shared selfishness,[5] loving the other not from Christian love, but loving the good feelings received from the other. Christian parents often fret about how their children will marry, and showing and teaching them such love offers much guidance that will lead toward healthy Christian marriage.

True Christian love will reveal itself in love for those 'neighbors' we rub shoulders with every day: the person behind us in the queue at the grocery, the driver of the slow-moving car in front of us, and the obnoxious child seated next to our child in the classroom. Above all, we and our children will evidence in our thoughts, feelings, and behavior how much we truly love the Lord our God.

Threats to Love

The early 21st Century is not an easy time to love as Jesus loves. Many things in the current world militate against teaching our children to love and having them receptive to the Spirit's ministering this fruit in their lives. I would like to examine two aspects of our day that threaten to stain the lives of our children and undermine love: the self-centered culture and selfish relationships.

THE CULTURE OF SELF

We opened this chapter with the selfish children at the Wonka chocolate factory, and have alluded several times already to the imminent danger posed by Western society's dramatic focus on the self as opposed to community. We will now look at this a bit more closely.

The media constantly preach that we should live for ourselves. The content of most movies and television shows implicitly promote and assume this view. A sitcom episode I recently viewed was about the death of a father's boss. When the man's children heard of the death, they initially were completely disinterested and unconcerned. Upon learning the funeral was during school hours, the boys feigned sadness in an effort to get out of school for a day. We were invited to laugh as we assume children would care more about the personal pleasure of getting out of schoolwork than about the death of a person made in God's image. Movies such as *Home Alone* and its successors falsely encourage small children to view adults as inept and so challenge them to be self-sufficient, taking care of themselves without expecting help from adults.

Advertising is a major perpetrator of selfism. 'Have it your way.' 'Just do it.' 'You deserve a break today.' 'You are worth it.' These messages blast our children's minds literally hundreds of times per day. Think of it. Not only do they see commercials while watching television, they see them on most Internet pages, hear them on the radio, ogle them in magazines and newspapers, and on billboards and signs in nearly every public place. Go to a movie, and you face ads and then previews so by the time you see the movie you came for, your child has been told she's not cool if she doesn't see five more. If that were not enough, the brand name on our clothes is ever more prominently displayed, making children walking advertisements. Some clothes are all the more desirable simply because of the designer name (read: advertisement) on them. Some two year olds are already committed to a certain brand of diapers because it depicts a favorite media character on it. Each ad carries the message

59

that you are not happy without their product, and since your happiness is the focus of life, you need their product. So our children plan their wish lists, rarely doubting that wanting more is good, and even more rarely giving thought to their neighbors who are poor and needy.

Selfism brings with it a leveling of authority. If each individual is autonomous, there is no overarching authority to which one yields her way. This sabotages the biblical authority of parents, church leaders, teachers, and so forth, and opens the door to the moral mantra of our time, tolerance. Each person is qualified and free to make up his own mind on things, whether it be religion or politics, and to say that is wrong is to be intolerant. Tolerance tolerates all things except intolerance. Who are you to think your views are right in some ultimate sense? Postmodernism teaches us there is no objective truth except for the truth that there is no truth.

These ideas seep into Christendom through efforts to be contemporary in our thinking. Christians want to love Jesus, but not to be divisive by having particular beliefs about him. After all, doctrine divides, and who are we to think we are right? The result is a quickening drift from the doctrinal faith established in the New Testament. No longer do we question unorthodox doctrines while still loving the person holding them (though this is closer to the true meaning of tolerance). Rather, we dilute our beliefs while they do the same, leading to fuzzy ideas of the faith that are inoffensive. So much for the 'offense of the cross'.

Our children readily catch on to this, and Christian Smith illustrates this well in the findings of the US National Study of Youth and Religion.[6] This extensive survey showed that most American teenagers see religion as rather important in their lives. Yet, Smith observes, 'American youth, like American adults, are nearly without exception profoundly individualistic, instinctively presuming autonomous, individual self-direction to be a universal human norm and life goal.'[7] How does this work out in their faith? Smith cites three implications.

First, he found in his research that most teens do not think anyone is required to do anything particular in his life, and religion is one of these areas where a person is free to do what she wants. Christianity is 'right' for most of these teens as individuals, but certainly not something others should be encouraged to adopt. Second, most teens are 'allergic' to anything they view as trying to influence them. They (naively) believe they decide their views independent of other influences because influencing is not respecting individuality. Smith sees this as also explaining why teens don't see their faith as influencing their lives...it is more of something they own by choice than a power that would influence them. Finally, this individualism means American teens embrace a view that vilifies judging others for being different. The Christian faith may be good for oneself, but it should never be seen as authoritative over the views of another.

This type of thinking implodes the notion of love as caring whether the other person has genuine Christian faith. We've seen how this ethos prevents many parents from calling their children's behavior wrong and correcting it as they have been led to believe tolerance for the child's behavior is how to show love. And, we've seen that actual research has shown this view to be false. Now, we must prevent our children from adapting this individualistic view. The Christian faith is authoritative. It involves surrender to Christ and a life of obedience. It teaches that God will judge others by his standards, and unpleasant consequences are certain if they do not repent and follow Christ. Being indifferent to the spiritual well-being of others is absolutely inconsistent with biblical love. It is true some have tried to 'hammer' others with the faith, but this excess does not excuse us from lovingly reaching out to others and exhorting them to faith.

Selfism thus threatens our children by persuading them that they are the authorities, not God. This encourages selfish behavior and consumption of goods that precludes giving to the poor. It also emasculates the content of the faith, calling our children to believe their choice is what matters. Since their faith is only a personal preference, it carries little moral weight and clearly prevents imposing their religion on others. We must confront this problem by demonstrating love that disciplines and by teaching how the Bible differs from the philosophy of the day.

We have seen how many relationships are built on self-love where both parties find mutual satisfaction from the other. But relationships built on this stretch of sand crumble when one partner (or both) no longer gratifies the self-love of the other.

Nowhere is this as evident as in the increase in divorces. In 1998, there were 1.1 million divorces in the US and in 2001 there were 160,000 in the United Kingdom and 55,300 in Australia.[8] In the US, more than one million children experience the divorce of their parents each year.[9] We see that many, many children suffer through the tragic divorce of their parents, and are put at considerably greater risk for mental health problems as a result.[10] Great numbers of little ones experience the absence of a parent, the constant shuffling back and forth on visits to the noncustodial parent, and the frequent ongoing tension between the two people they love most. It is no wonder they struggle to understand what genuine love looks like. Christian homes are by no means immune from this epidemic of failed marriages as the strong biblical teachings about the permanence of marriage are discarded for a chance at self-fulfillment. While there are terrible situations where godly men or women grieve through a divorce forced upon them by spouses who are cruel, adulterous, and even brutal, most marriages fail because the parents lack the type of love for each other that we have examined in this chapter.

Our churches must seriously confront this issue. We must promote the sanctity of marriage, yet provide support and restoration for divorced persons. We must creatively find ways to minister to the children impacted by these broken marriages and show them healthy love in the congregation. Divorced parents must openly discuss the situation with their children, admit where they have failed, ask forgiveness where appropriate, and reiterate the nature of love as taught in Scripture.

Another relational threat to our children is the aggressive pursuit of pleasure and success that consume parents. Workaholism sometimes not only affects one, but both parents. Replacing 'quantity' time with 'quality' time does little to change our children's impression that our careers or money are more important than relationship. Even our time at home may reflect this, as we bow before the altar of the sacred video screen rather than actually relate to family members. This approach to life leaves parents irritable and often modeling ways of coping with life that are not rooted in Scripture. Children, especially young children, watch and learn. 'No scientist ever looked through a microscope more intently than the average child who observes her family day in and night out,' conclude the authors of a major research project on children.[11] Even if divorce is not at issue, parents who desire loving children must model loving relationships.

The self-focused type of love underlies the new tradition of 'church-hopping'. It is rare for children to grow in one community and know only one church family for their years of minority. Moves are sometimes necessary due to relocation of the family or to unbiblical changes in a church making a move a matter of conscience. However, most often, families move from church to church in an effort to satisfy their selfish tastes. Many churches even deliberately appeal to this in an effort to solicit new attendees. Worship serves to soothe the senses more than offer worship to the King. Taste, not Scripture, dictates the style and content of worship. If the style isn't right, the family moves to another church with one they like better. In the process, children do not see committed love working in community. We see the sacrifices the church made for one another throughout the book of Acts, yet we see only faint reflections of this in most of our churches today. We must prayerfully reflect on this fact as parents and reconsider what our church attending patterns teach our children. We must consider this as church leaders and seek God's face on how to be community in an individualistic age as this will impact families in far greater ways than our worship styles.

The culture of the self is also promoted in our homes in subtle ways that train us in the world's way of thinking. What is the harm of dining out frequently, entertaining ourselves incessantly, and spending our money at will? We have tithed, haven't we? God got his due. We had our devotions today, didn't we? We've done more for our faith than most of the folks at our church. So, what is the problem?

The problem is this looks very little like the life of Jesus or even Paul. Certainly there are times for refreshment and celebration, but we often live our lives as though others are just fine and so we feel free to indulge ourselves. Yet, our Lord did not worry about money, his career, or having a good time. He was on a definite mission that shaped his use of time and resources. He reached out to the poor, sick, and even children. His times alone were not vacations at the beach, but prayer retreats. Paul, too, demonstrates the point. He made tents, but not to finance a house and classy clothes. He earned his money to support his Christian calling to spread the gospel.

It is not so much that entertainment is in itself wrong. We need breaks. But, we see ourselves working to support our entertainment and thus do not consider the poor and needy around us. Our work is also to finance our ministry for Christ. Occasional refreshment strengthens us for the work, but the focus of our lives is service to God and others. When we watch television or the latest DVD, the question is what else might we be doing. When entertainment is an end in itself, it changes its function from relaxing diversion to a focus of life. It then replaces love of others. What else might you be doing if you were not watching television? Getting to know your neighbors? Serving food at a homeless shelter? Writing notes of encouragement to missionaries? Praying together as a family? The opportunity lost is more the problem than the entertainment itself. We must reach out in love to others in fulfillment of the Great Commandment, and as a way of teaching our children to do the same. Surrendering to the culture of the self will stain our efforts to raise spiritually fruitful children.

So we see more completely now how societal trends conspire to produce self-centered children like the ones Willy Wonka met. We are challenged prayerfully to do battle against these influences and actively to promote genuinely Christian love in our families, for the sake of Christ, and for the benefit of our children.

Practically Promoting Love

While I have offered some practical suggestions throughout the chapter, I'll conclude with a few more for children of differing ages.

PRESCHOOL CHILDREN

Read them stories of loving people and deeds from the Bible and other sources. Point out unloving acts in other stories that you read to them and that they see or hear through media.

Teach giving from an early age. Have young children draw pictures or make simple crafts for grandparents, neighbors, or older people at your church.

Select a missionary family, get pictures, and pray with your child for this family. This may even be better if the missionary family has kids. Focus your prayers on asking God to produce the fruit of the Spirit in their children.

Monitor your children's play with other children, actively instructing them on sharing while teaching them to have empathy for the feelings of others.

Limit exposure to commercials, and explain to children the motives of advertisers from early on. Teach your children to be skeptical about commercialism.

ELEMENTARY CHILDREN

Do a study during family devotions or worship on caring for others and why this would please God. Illustrate with Scriptural examples such as the story of the Good Samaritan (told originally, if you recall, to answer who one's neighbor is).

Closely monitor their media consumption and its content. Severely restrict, if not eliminate, violent video games and movies. Beware 'addiction' even to games that are not overtly immoral.

Encourage interaction with others during free time. Play games as a family, get the child out in the neighborhood with other children, and invite friends over to the house for structured activities, not staring at a television set.

Involve your children in a regular community service activity to teach caring for others as a focus of life. Ideally, they join you in a ministry that you are already involved in.

Frequently discuss God's love for your children and ways he has shown it.

TEENAGERS

Have the teen critique movies and television programs as to the character of the protagonists, and how these stack up against the biblical notion of love. Pay particular attention to how romantic love is portrayed.

In a similar fashion, move from 'preaching' love to them to asking them questions that encourage them to think through the biblical teachings for themselves. What should love look like in this situation? How might selfish motives be evident in a certain relationship? And so forth.

Encourage your teens to have a volunteer job helping others. It can be as simple as cleaning up trash from the streets of the neighborhood once a month. Other options might be volunteering at a hospital, an animal shelter, a church, or other community organization.

Openly discuss the qualities of their friendships. Help them learn to think through why they are attracted to certain persons, and to stack these reasons up against biblical love.

Expose them to good examples of love. If there is a young adult you know who illustrates love, ask them to be a mentor to your teen. Find godly peers for them to associate with and learn from. As they look more to others in the teen years, see that their role models are individuals who love God.

And for all children, pray for their protection, and for their growth in the Spirit's fruit of love.

5

PURSUING HAPPINESS OR SAVORING JOY?

It's every child's fantasy come true. The ultimate vacation experience. The height of ecstasy. The mother lode of happiness. Walt Disney World. It is truly a surreal experience, like stepping into a cartoon. It isn't just rides. It is a complete wonderland, filled with castles, giant tree houses, spaceships, and most anything you can imagine. Those children's icons, the Disney characters, patrol the immaculately kept grounds. These characters-come-to-life will even join you for a meal. The cares of the world recede and dreams become reality. Surely this is true joy for a child.

Or maybe not. Several years ago I had occasion to visit Mickey's wonderland, and what a treat for a psychologist! Watching the people was more fascinating than seeing the exhibits. Look there, a little boy of about six, wearing his Goofy ears and designer clothes, his mother frantically trying to keep the deluxe ice cream from staining them. Rapturous delight? Hardly. The little boy is screaming in anger and frustration because he has been told 'no' to purchasing yet another souvenir. And over there, a girl of about twelve. Stylishly (though immodestly) dressed with tinted hair and conspicuous jewelry, her efforts to look 'cool' are offset by the scowl on her face. Happy she is not. One needn't be intrusive to see that she is offended by her parents' denying her the right to call friends on her cell phone. And at a nearby table sits a family of four, staring blankly into space as they sip their sodas through souvenir straws. If I ever saw boredom, this was it. Our friend Veruca Salt would have been quite at home.

In a sense, I was surprised by the amount of unhappiness I witnessed at this alleged haven of joy; but in another way, I was not. Disneyworld is the epitome of what the world says should make us happy. Everything there cries out to enjoy oneself, to indulge, experience, and escape the doldrums of day-to-day life. It would be the perfect place to fulfill the pursuit of happiness if current ideas of happiness are correct. Scripture, of course, teaches us they are not.

The desire for happiness is universal, being viewed as so basic to human existence that seeking happiness is an assumed right according to the United States Declaration of Independence. Typically this happiness is identified with pleasure, doing what we enjoy. And most often we are taught that these things are not part of routine life. 'Live for the weekend' is the adult version— work hard for five days to earn money to do fun stuff on the weekend. During most of history, and even today across most parts of the world, making enough money to survive was the goal. But in the postmodern West, entertainment is a necessity as this is what we are told will make us happy. So, our children are growing into this world and have more things to entertain them than any generation in history. The result is we have a chronically bored and unhappy generation. How can that be?

Most Christians intuitively know that joy is different from happiness, but more than we like to think, we are drawn along with the world into the pursuit of transient pleasures, believing these will bring us the joy our hearts long for. Our children see this thinking in our lives while the consumerist culture screams it at them at every turn. The notion that constant entertainment will satisfy us becomes so much a part of our lives that we fail to see it.

As we examine the wonderful biblical notion of joy as a fruit of the Spirit in this chapter, we will look more closely at why happiness bores our children. We will examine the biblical teachings about joy and see how even psychology is affirming a path with which we are unaccustomed. We will again conclude with some practical suggestions for protecting our children from false ideas of happiness and for directing them to true Spiritual joy.

Bored by Happiness

Let's trace the development of the current epidemic unhappiness among our children along the lines of some of the common types of entertainment.

Go back a mere 100 years, and imagine how different life was. What would a child do in the afternoons? She might have chores, help her mother make dinner, or play outside. A boy might have different chores to do, yet children felt needed in the economy of the family. Electric light was available, but what might a family do in the evening after a hard day at work or school? Maybe talk to each other? Read? Take a walk? Simply get more rest?

Then came radio. Stop for a moment and ponder. Even though radio programming put everyone together in a room to listen, and the programming was not morally offensive at the time, consider what was lost. An overlooked problem with entertainment as the path to happiness is how it replaces activities that are more inherently joyful. Many parents still have fond memories of cooking with their mothers (or fathers!), or working as a family to fix up the house or to move to a new one. Entertainment like radio may keep the family in the same room, but something is lost in the change from interacting with one another in constructive and productive ways.

Radio soon gave way to television, and dramatic changes followed. My parents grew up with a radio. My childhood was marked by three channels of black-and-white television. My daughter's early years were marked by the option of multitudes of cable channels including several devoted to so-called children's programming 24 hours a day. The technology has made great progress, but viewing options haven't made children happier. The convenience of television in children's rooms makes memorable family times even harder to come by.

One hundred years ago, children played games outdoors. No need for hundreds of dollars' worth of equipment; a ball of string, a ball, or a patch of woods would do. Children used their creativity to play, and found happiness in so doing. Toy manufacturing progressed, and many more options became available, though these restricted creativity. Then came the watershed day. I remember as a child going to the airport and waiting for my father's flight to arrive. Looking around, I saw a new item: a game with a TV screen. I played, and was exhilarated to try to block a round blip from going past a short dash on the side of the screen, this being my 'paddle' in the game of Pong. Great fun. A generation later, children play video games on hand-held devices with graphics that are startlingly realistic. And so is the content of many of these games. From the innocence of table tennis we now have games where you can kill, mutilate, cannibalize, and rape. What does it mean that we consider these things entertainment? And where did the neighborhood game of football go?

Then there are movies. The early ones were black and white, silent events. What a treat to go to the occasional movie at the theater. Then came color, powerful sound systems, Cinerama, even 3-D. But going to a theater was expensive, time-consuming, and inconvenient. Enter videotaped movies which add the convenience of owning your favorite movies even as it takes away the social event of an evening at the theater. Whereas you might have seen a movie several times in a theater if you really liked it, now you can watch even mediocre ones until you memorize them (talk to a few children and you'll see, they're pretty close to having the dialogue of their favorites perfected). Videos became DVD's, even more visually stunning and even more portable. Now your children can watch them in your car...possibly on a built in player. Thus movies become ubiquitous. Entertainment is omnipresent. And whatever message it is carrying is being drilled into our children's heads more frequently than their multiplication facts. But maybe even more critically, interacting with family has almost disappeared into the thick fog of constant entertainment.

Much the same history could be traced with music. Ipods adorn our children now, highly portable and personal as no longer do you need to buy albums, you simply download your favorite tracks. Powerful, hearing-threatening earphones aim the high fidelity sound at vulnerable eardrums, drowning out the sounds of nearby people. The fun never stops, even though the fun becomes increasingly individualistic, excluding both friends and family.

But friends are still important to children. People used to walk to visit their friends. Then parents would drive them, or they could talk on the phone...anywhere with a cell phone. Email made worldwide communication immediate, but instant messaging was even faster and more readily lent itself to group discussion. Now children clamor for their own blog site, and keep track of their friends via Internet postings. All of this is cool and keeps young minds busy, but it doesn't lend itself to genuine relationships, or happiness—much less godliness.

Finally, shopping is a favorite way to try to find happiness. As the cute little motto quips, 'When the going gets tough, the tough go shopping.' Shopping is rarely to get necessities, but the fleeting delight of a purchase becomes a form of entertainment. Clever retailers know this as shopping malls and the stores in them become more like amusement parks than simply markets. Carousel rides, bungee experiences, and even roller coasters add to the fun of going to the mall. Video screens stimulate at every turn. And still our children are bored. Consider fast food and other restaurants. The irony of McDonald's 'happy meals' for kids can't be missed. The entertainment and consumption value of the toy is what children want. Now restaurants even need a playground to sell hamburgers. Adult restaurants are no better, as television screens distract from conversation among diners.

Boredom is spiked with bitterness as all of these entertainments are foisted on our children as the way to be happy. The increasingly aggressive advertising industry sees to it that this lie is perpetuated. People who are content don't spend as much money and thus hurt the economy. The irony here is that advertisements must convince us we are not happy, and to gain the elusive happiness, we need their product. Once we get it, not only does it fail to satisfy, but another commercial reminds us we need still more 'stuff' to find joy. In fact, the never-ending increase in the 'edginess' of media needed to keep an audience betrays the fact that entertainment and 'stuff' do not satisfy. Why are believers sucked into this whirlpool that never delivers what it offers?

71

The Fallacy of the Pursuit of Happiness

Let us consider how we become part of this futile pursuit of happiness and unintentionally draw our children into it. First, we are deceived by the way our culture uses words and alters meaning. Take the word 'amusement'. The early meaning of the word 'amuse' was to stare stupidly, the idea being to distract from the important things of life. One can see a place for such as there is a time to refresh our minds and lay down our concerns to be refreshed. But like halftime of a football match, the refreshment is to ready us for the important things. Our culture sadly makes amusement itself the important thing, minimizing the significance of our daily work and activities. For a believer, amusement is better seen as a brief 'leave' for a soldier at war. A respite is given to keep fresh for the battle itself. An army who is always on leave will not be effective, nor are Christians who live for amusement and not for the battle for the Kingdom of God. Thus, parents are raising soldiers, not consumers of amusement.

Then there is 'entertainment'. It really means to hold the attention with something distracting or amusing (remember what that means!). One can consider the ideas in past times of entertaining a weary traveler, the notion being that warm hospitality would renew the traveler from the journey and for the rest of the journey. It is a means to an end, not an end in itself. This is what has changed today. Entertainment dominates many lives and is the purpose of life for many. As we mentioned, that's great for the economy as you need the latest high definition television and music device to stay entertained. But this betrays the real issue that life itself has no meaning and the day's work serves no purpose other than to finance the entertainment to follow. Follow this closely. This thinking quietly admits that life is meaningless, and so amusement is all there is. When a Christian lives this way, it raises serious questions about her understanding of her faith. And what does it communicate to a child in a Christian home when we live as though entertainment (even Christian entertainment) is what it's all about?

This philosophy of life leaves people without goals other than distraction. One works not as a calling or ministry or service, but as a necessary evil to purchase distraction from meaninglessness. Thousands of years later, the insights of Ecclesiastes hold true. All this is vanity and there is nothing new under the sun…just better technology to deliver dissatisfaction.

The vain pursuit of pleasure in 'fun' or entertainment fails because it misses what true joy is. Once we accept that we find joy in fleeting pleasureful activities, we miss the opportunity for joy as a basic disposition of life. Joy is then excluded from daily tasks that comprise most of our lives. We can have moments of happiness, but not an ongoing joy in life.

J. I. Packer sees this trend among believers in what he calls 'hot tub religion'. He observes that it misses the mark as 'the paradoxical truth is to seek pleasure, comfort, and happiness is to guarantee that you will miss them all.'[1] he concludes that joy does not depend on pleasure, concurring with Ecclesiastes 2: 1–11 that pleasure-seeking brings only boredom and disgust. Pleasures themselves serve as pointers to God and are good, but the problem arises when they are viewed as ends in themselves and supplant the deeper Christian virtue of joy.

Again, much of the blame lies in modern psychology which has taught our generation to pursue pleasure in self-gratification. Yet, recent psychological research in what is termed positive psychology is changing psychologists' understanding of where 'pleasure' really lies. Let me share two examples to illustrate.

Martin Seligman is one of the major names in modern psychology, and he learned some interesting things about feeling good from his students. He gave his University of Pennsylvania students two assignments one week. They were to indulge themselves in an activity they thought was fun such as a night out with friends, going to a movie, or the like. That week they also were intentionally to do something to help another person, such as visit a nursing home, serve at a soup kitchen, or the like. He then had his students complete surveys about the experiences. The result? The students actually felt better when doing for others than when indulging themselves. Strangely, more happiness is found in acts of kindness than in doing what we are taught is fun. I wonder if our children realize that, or have had the chance Seligman's students did to see the difference as their parents take them along on missions of service to others. My daughter happily remembers accompanying me when she was little as I delivered baskets of goodies to the widows of our church. The delight on the faces of those women was reflected in my daughter's joy in helping bring that delight.

The second example from secular psychology comes from the work of Mikaly Czikszentmihalyi (tough name, isn't it?). His work is based on figuring out where people find the greatest pleasure, and it resulted in a concept he calls 'flow'. His research found that people find their greatest pleasure when engaged in a task that moderately challenges their skills and is goal oriented. These produce 'flow' where the person feels almost lost in time and is aware of little else besides the activity. This explains the attraction, for instance, of rock climbers. Why do something that is dangerous and hard work as well? It produces flow as you pursue the top of the hillside and test your strength and skills. Flow can also be found in more mundane activities such as working on a craft project or writing. Interestingly, most incidences of flow occur during the course on one's work, disproving the 'live for the weekend' philosophy of life.

Secular psychology concedes that happiness is discovered in work and acts of kindness more than the direct pursuit of pleasure. Christians should not be surprised. The prospect of joy strengthened Jesus to endure the cross (Heb. 12: 1–2), certainly a great work and an incomparable kindness to us.

All of this reveals how deceived many believers are as to what will bring happiness and joy. The culture indoctrinates us and our children in lies as to what will fulfill us, using this to take our money while leaving us bitter, unfulfilled, and simply bored. Seeing the problem is the first step in overcoming it. As we reject this worldly enticement to be entertained, let us examine the Word of God to learn of true joy.

Joy in the Bible

As Christian, we of course know that the Bible is the source of knowledge for our lives. Yet, we must admit we must make time, sit down, open it, and prayerfully read what it says, unlike the media that blare at us from every corner. If we are to move past the message of the world to the message of the Word, we must be deliberate in tuning out the culture and taking time to consider the biblical message. This is where the road to joy for us and for our children begins. A brief survey of joy in the Bible produces a few important themes for us to reflect on.

A JOYFUL HEART IS GOOD MEDICINE (PROVERBS 17: 22)

Modern psychological research only proves what the Bible has long taught about the health benefits of joy. People who are 'happy' as a trait (not just when doing something 'fun') get sick less, recover from surgery more quickly, and in general enjoy greater health than less happy persons. Depression is an obvious lack of joy and depression is increasing in our day, especially among children. The loss of joy has a cost and to recover it is to promote health. That, of course, is not the final goal, but it shows how joy can sustain our bodies through tough times of adversity.

SPIRITUAL JOY IS GREATER THAN WORLDLY JOY

Psalm 16: 11 tells us that only in God's presence is fullness of joy and pleasures forevermore. What earthly joys can compare! That is true now as we worship the Lord, but even more so when we are with him in heaven. This joy is far greater than material wealth brings (Ps. 4: 7). Look at the lives of the rich, and you see that they are no happier than others. Psychological research actually shows that, once you are above the poverty level, more money does not make for more happiness. Much greater is the joy that comes as a fruit of the Spirit who gives us faith in God (Ps. 15: 11; 37: 4; 42: 1–2; 63: 1; 34: 8; 36: 8; 119: 103).

WE FIND JOY IN OBEYING GOD

Scripture is almost circular at this point. God is to be served in joy but serving God yields joy. Deuteronomy 28: 45–8 threatens curses to Israel and her descendents because they did not serve God with joyfulness and gladness of heart, suggesting even obedience done with a frown does not satisfy God. Most parents know what this is like as we've had our children do as we say while pouting as they do so. This does not satisfy us nor honor us, so why would our pouty obedience please and honor a holy God?

Something is wrong when this occurs, for genuine obedience produces joy. Jesus taught that his words impart his joy to us (John 15: 11). Standing firm in the faith brings joy (2 Cor. 1: 24), a joy that no one can take away (John 16: 22). Paul's ministry aimed to produce 'progress and joy in the faith' (Phil. 1: 25), and he prayed for the strength of his flocks so they would endure with joy (Colossians 1: 11). Indeed, the whole aim of God's kingdom and our kingdom obedience is not eating and drinking (physical pleasures) but righteousness (the fruit of obedience), peace, and joy in the Holy Spirit (Rom. 14: 17). This makes sense, for God himself is perfect joy, and obedience makes us more like him and thus able to know more of his joy.

Scripture is filled with examples of joyful obedience. Romans 12: 8 anticipates the work of Seligman discussed earlier as it speaks of doing acts of mercy with cheerfulness. We are so caught up in the joy of our master (Matt. 25: 21, 23) that we sell our worldly interests (Matt. 13: 44). Thus, giving is joyful (2 Cor. 9: 7) even to where we rejoice in suffering loss for the sake of others (Heb. 10: 34). We serve others eagerly (1 Pet. 5: 2) even as we allow our spiritual leaders to watch over our own souls with joy (Heb. 13: 17).

The spiritual progress of those to whom we minister also brings us joy. Paul called the Philippian Christians his 'joy and crown' (4: 1), and John concurred, 'I have no greater joy than to hear that my children are walking in truth' (3 John 1: 4). He, of course, was referring to his spiritual children, but how true this is also of our physical children. Their obedience is a source of great joy to their parents.

This scriptural theme makes clear that seeking happiness in the world is misguided, and as we learn to obey God, and to teach our children to do the same, we become caught up in the joy of God and his people. But this is an 'acquired taste', acquired by walking with God in the newness of life given in regeneration. We learn it as we exercise faith, and we must guide our children into the same, seeking God's grace to open their eyes to this wonderful truth.

SIN STEALS OUR JOY

This naturally follows from what we just considered. If joy is in obeying God and fellowshipping with him, sin will take this joy away. David knew that in the magnificent penitential Psalm 51 as he prayed for God to restore the joy of his salvation (v. 12) after he had sinned. Psalm 30: 5 acknowledges God will sometimes be angry with our sin, yet 'weeping may tarry for the night, but joy comes in the morning.' He is committed to our joy as we are committed to obeying such a loving Father. Sin turns dancing to mourning (Lam. 5: 15) but God's promise is to turn mourning to dancing (Jer. 31: 13) as even in our sinful failures we look to a gracious God for forgiveness.

As a parent rejoices in obedient children, so rebellious children drain away a parent's joy (Prov. 17: 21). As Christian parents, our joy is inextricably bound up in the spiritual lives of our children. Our fight for their joy in Christ is a fight for our joy as well.

TRUE JOY ENDURES AFFLICTION

Biblical belief departs dramatically from cultural ideas at this point. We are taught to avoid any suffering or hardship. Think of how many innovations are designed to give us more comfort with the idea being that will make us happier. Have you ever told your children of the 'bad ole' days' when one had to actually get up, walk to the television, and change the channels by turning a knob on the set? The remote control is such a part of life that such effort now seems monumental. We have been convinced that any inconvenience, much less any actual suffering, will detract from our happiness and so should be avoided at all costs.

But compare the words of Scripture. Paul exults that 'in all our affliction, I am overflowing with joy' (2 Cor. 7: 4). Shortly after that, he praises the churches in Macedonia who amidst affliction and poverty had an 'abundance of joy' that overflowed into generosity (2 Cor. 8: 2). The Thessalonians also draw praise, for they 'received the word in much affliction, with the joy of the Holy Spirit' (1 Thess. 1: 6). Then James (1: 2)

77

adds that we are to 'count it all joy…when [we] meet trials of various kinds.'

Here we begin to see the secret to joy that is deep within our souls and not at the mercy of the whims of life. Our joy is in God and in following him. Knowing we are his and that he is building his kingdom is our joy. Even adversity is not threatening because we know it is God at work. Like an athlete forced to practice diligently by a coach, we know the suffering only makes us better. Or, paraphrasing a sign I spied recently, calm seas do not make for skilled sailors. We endure knowing our Lord will win the day, and is causing all things to work together for good (Rom. 8: 28). We know we will not be forsaken (Heb. 13: 5), and we cannot be separated from the love of God (Rom. 8: 35–9) no matter what. When our joy is rooted in the Fount of all joy, it is unshakable in good times or bad.

Enjoying God

Let's pull these themes together to direct us to the joy for which we hunger, and which we long to see in our children. First, a word on words. We saw the etymology of entertainment and amusement earlier. What of 'enjoy'? It actually means 'to rejoice in'. It implies joy is focused on something outside ourselves more than just a feeling we have. Clearly this is the case in the famous opening of the *Westminster Shorter Catechism* which states that 'the chief end of man is to glorify God and enjoy him forever'. The idea is that the Christian, fulfilling the goal of being human, finds joy in God. Here is a strange thought for our day. How many of us can honestly say we take great joy in God—in thinking of him, reading his Word, praying to him, and worshipping him? Worship is often focused on entertaining us with music rather than our joy existing in our knowledge of and relationship to God. The music helps us to express the joy already within us. This contrasts with what we often see in church. People arrive looking rather unhappy, perk up with the music, then leave much the same way they came.

John Piper, in one of the most influential books in my walk with Christ,[2] thinks this catechism answer might be better expressed as the chief end of man being to glorify God by enjoying him forever. What does he mean by this? Piper believes humans all are driven to find happiness, agreeing with much of what we said earlier. However, he also maintains the person, thing, or activity that brings you the greatest pleasure most betrays the god of your heart. So, if one is so committed to a sports team that he is ecstatic after a win or inconsolable after a loss, that sports team is his god. Or, if one loves a television program so much that she rushes through prayer time to see it, it may be her god. If we take our greatest joy in God as we ought, we are truly glorifying him as God. It only makes sense that the greatest joy should come from the greatest Being. In contrast, most of us spend our days seeking joy in passing pleasures and possessions that will never fulfill. Piper quotes C. S. Lewis who said we are like ignorant children who go on making mud pies in a slum because we cannot appreciate the offer of a holiday at the sea. If we as parents are guilty, how are we to direct our children to such joy?

First, we must understand this joy. This is not a joy in experiencing God's blessings, for that is to rejoice in the gifts more than the Giver. These gifts are wonderful and praiseworthy, but they fade in the glory of the Giver himself. Just as I cherish gifts from my wife, I would never trade them for knowing her and enjoying her company. I fear this is one place we train our children incorrectly. We love God not because he will give us good parking places, or a nice job, or a girlfriend, or money, or health. We love God because he is God, and thus the loveliest thing in the universe.

But this is an acquired taste. God gives us joy early in our Christian lives, but this grows as we contemplate him in his Word and as we see his sovereign hand in our daily lives. We increasingly know and marvel at him as we walk with him. This is why obedience brings joy, and even explains how suffering can increase joy as Jesus modeled for us (Heb. 12: 1–2). We learn that enjoying God means knowing he is in control and accomplishing his purposes regardless of the ups and downs of our lives. Joy then in rooted in an unchanging God, not transient circumstances. Yet, we will not grow in the joy of God if we do not realize it is in him our happiness lies. We must surrender pursuit of earthly pleasures and the distorted theologies that tell us God is good only because he multiplies

79

our earthly entertainments. We must be directed to God as the true Fount of joy, and guide our children to this knowledge as well. And this means teaching them the vanity of chasing earthly pleasures…in our words and in our lives.

Unlike the passing pleasures of the world, such joy comes from a spiritual battle, being the Spirit's gift to us in our combat with the world. As such, it is able to persevere in suffering and hardships because it rests in the God who is bringing in his kingdom and will not be stopped by the powers of the world. It is a battle for true joy, and one into which we are to initiate our children. It begins with exposing the falsehoods of the Disneyland approach to happiness, and ends in aiming our children to the Fount of every blessing to find the true joy the Spirit gives.

The Fight for Our Children's Joy

John Piper's book includes a very helpful appendix that lists 15 pointers on how to fight for joy. For our application section, I will list these and offer suggestions on how to use these in the lives of the children we love.

> Realize that authentic joy in God is a gift (Ps. 51: 12). We love techniques, the five easy steps to this or that. But joy is a gift, a fruit of the Spirit of God, and thus not subject to being produced at will. Pray diligently for your children to take joy in God and for that joy to overrule the passing pleasures of the world.

> Realize that joy must be fought for relentlessly (2 Cor. 1: 24). Prayer is part of this fight, but it encompasses our efforts to train and guide our children in a culture that is contrary to joy. It involves effort and foregoing more immediate pleasures in pursuit of the true joy found in Christ.

> Resolve to attack all known sin in your life (Rom. 6: 11–13). I often say to parents with whom I work that you are no better parent than you are a person, and your victory over sin will impact the lives of your children. Encourage your children

to battle sin in their lives. The self-esteem movement has left many parents afraid of actually confronting children's wrongdoing lest it hurt their self-esteem. This is shallow and erroneous. Pray with your children over sin, and praise them when you see signs they are battling this great enemy.

Learn the secret of gutsy guilt: fight like a justified sinner (Mic. 7: 8–9). Teach your children not to fear facing their failures. Irresponsibility is rampant today, and it is not becoming for Christians. Though we sin, we can face it fearlessly knowing we are made just in Christ. Model this and guide your children to deal with sins the same. Just as a musician who refuses to face mistakes won't improve, so the believer who hides from sin won't find joy.

Realize that the battle is primarily a fight to see God for who he is (Ps. 34: 8). Young children see God best in Bible stories, though the reader needs to take care to point to the God who is controlling the 'action' so even young children see joy in God as the Bible portrays him, not as described in popular culture. This may mean as parents we need to think more deeply about who God really is, maybe even studying a little theology ourselves. J. I. Packer's *Knowing God* is a wonderful place to start.

Meditate on the Word of God day and night (Ps. 19: 8). This argues for the importance of family worship where the parents think through the implications of Scripture for young children and teach grade school children and teenagers to do the same for themselves. Once again, it will be difficult to teach what we don't know, so here is a challenge to parents to practice this skill. Children who love video games will gladly spend hours seeking to understand them better, so why would a true believer not spend time thinking about God's Word as a source of genuine joy.

Pray earnestly and continually for an inclination for God (Ps. 85: 6). How often do our children hear us pray such a prayer where we ask to hunger and thirst more for God? Where will

81

they learn it if not from us? Show them how to pray this way, encourage them to do the same, and pray fervently that they will long for God more than for the dainties of the world.

Learn to preach to yourself rather than listen to yourself (Ps. 42: 5). Although there is a place for learning to listen to yourself, we seem to be encouraged to know and 'go with' our feelings at every turn by the pop psychology messages of our day. Instead, we must train our children to challenge their feelings with such 'preaching', refusing to be 'cast down' by circumstances as we are reminded to 'hope in God'. We, as those who care for children, are easily prey to discouraging thoughts that fight against joy, and we must strengthen ourselves in this battle as we direct our children to do likewise.

Spend time with God-saturated people who help you see God and fight the fight (1 Sam. 23: 16). More than we like to think, our children's lives are shaped by those they are around. This is one reason why it is vital that churches afford occasion for children to be around adults of all ages who find joy in the Lord. The mature peace of an older saint can have a powerful influence on a child, making it critical that we see to it that our children are exposed to these saints in the church. Children are also naturally attracted to older children or teens, and we need to find ways for godly young people to mentor the little ones as well. This raises the issue of what types of children our little ones should be around in school, and, while this is not the place for a discussion of public versus private or home schooling, it demonstrates the prayerful consideration we need to give to who our children's friends are to be.

Be patient in the night of God's seeming absence (Ps. 40: 3). Just as any good coach pushes his players to be stronger through endurance, so God will in his wisdom bring times of darkness. Our 'instant society' forgets this, and we must teach our children difficult times are part of God's plan so that we can even rejoice in them as they shape us.

Get the rest, exercise, and proper diet that your body was designed by God to have (1 Cor. 6: 20). Easily, we and our children become portly from pursuing the passive pleasures of our pastimes. Though the fruit of joy need not depend on our physical health, we should not sabotage it by poor care for our bodies either. Keep children active in healthy ways. The best play is usually not done sitting down. Cultivate healthy tastes in food by restricting fast foods and other 'convenience' foods that trade brief bursts of good taste for inflated cholesterol counts.

Make a proper use of God's revelation in nature (Matt. 6: 26). In an electronic society, one must be deliberate in exposing children to nature. Trips to local parks, day hikes in the woods, and vacations to scenic areas instead of to commercial destinations allow children to see the wonders of nature. Watch a sunset and teach your children to thank their Heavenly Father who makes such art for us to enjoy. Even see God's great design in insects in the yard or unusual flowers. Do this enough, and children begin to see these joyful gifts of God on their own.

Read great books about God and biographies of great saints (Heb. 13: 7). I might add that there are even a few good videos about saints, such as the Luther movie several years ago. Still, books are preferable. Many such books are available in formats suitable to children, including those detailing the lives of missionaries. Heroes and heroines don't have to be television, music, or movie stars. Christian Focus Publications offers many quality resources in this area.

Do the hard and loving thing for the sake of others—witness and mercy (Isa. 58: 10–11). This is consistent with material from earlier in the chapter where we learned that serving others brings more joy than we think. This again requires initiative. Find an elderly neighbor and have your son mow her yard or your daughter clean her house. Volunteer at a reading clinic and have your children teach others. The opportunities are limited only by your creativity.

Get a global vision for the cause of Christ and pour yourself out for the unreached (Ps. 67: 1–2, 6–7). God's most conspicuous work in our day is in the Southern hemisphere as the cross marches forward in the two-thirds world. Identify missionaries and pray for them. Learn the names of their children and have your children pray specifically for them. One benefit of technology is email that allows your children to correspond quickly with many missionary children and learn of their lives and needs first-hand. Go as a family on a short-term missions trip to an area in your country or another one. Teenagers especially can offer meaningful service to others while tasting the joy in serving Christ and his kingdom. As we cultivate this different view of joy in the lives of our children and young people, the Spirit will prove faithful to grant joy to the children of God.

6

PEACE IN AN AGE OF INTENSITY

The look of misery on Jessica's face betrays her suffering. This nine-year-old girl is on the third day of a break from school, and is quite unhappy. Her mother is mystified, having expected her daughter to delight in her holiday. So she asks what the matter is. Jessica's reply is blunt and to the point, 'I'm bored!'

Jessica's mother is speechless as her mind races to try to understand this. Jessica has dozens of movies on DVD, an MP3 player, and 100 channels of cable television only a few pushes of a button away. She has Internet access to any games that she doesn't already have on her computer, and is proud owner of enough Barbie dolls to populate a small town. She even owns a large bookshelf full of unread books. How in the world can Jessica be bored? Shouldn't all of these resources for entertainment make her content?

Another lie of our times is exposed, as the answer for Jessica's mother is 'no'. The constant availability of highly stimulating activities is producing children who have little sense of contentment or peace. Most definitely, the same can be said of adults, too. We are like leaves caught up in a whirlpool, spinning faster and faster, but going in circles. Since everything around us is caught in the same whirlpool, we fail to see the changes this brings as the slow but steady trip downstream is interrupted by an increase in speed but a loss of direction. We move faster and faster, enamored of the excitement but having no sense of what we are really doing and why. Our speed keeps us distracted, but does not bring us peace.

The impact of such a whirlpool culture on children is profound. Unlike the 'flow' mentioned in the last chapter where the challenge of a goal brings happiness, the excitements of our world are pointless, mostly aiming at simply entertaining us for a few moments. Our children are trained from their earliest days to be stimulated in far more intense ways than previous generations have known, and it's easy to be caught up in this without noticing the consequences. Let's take a few moments to consider this.

The flashing of television screens, whether broadcast programs or DVDs, produces a mind-numbing sensation as the pulsing light tickles otherwise passive brains. The words of a book being read can't compete with the stimulation of a video screen. The patience of waiting for the mail carrier to arrive is replaced with instant messaging and email, again delivered via the flickering video screen. Even telephone calls fade in excitement compared to the multitasking of chatting with several friends online while simultaneously surfing the Internet. Music, too, moves from being soothing to shocking, with newer technologies making for more powerful bass lines and more intense guitar sounds. The startling power of the newer earphones has even caused long-term rock and roll stars to speak out to caution against their use. Movies are becoming more potent as improved special effects, imaging techniques, and sound systems make the theater experience more surreal than ever. We could easily take more time to describe the same in the workplace as information technology accelerates the pace of business frantically. James Gleick[1] had it right in his book *Faster* as he brought these dangers of an ever-accelerating world to our attention.

All of this intense excitement creates a new threshold for stimulation that is almost impossible to satisfy. Like a whirlpool, the pace of life moves faster and faster so something has to be exceptionally exciting to catch our eyes. This explains the constant need for television, music, and movies to be 'edgier' to compete: we quickly acclimatize to a level of stimulation, requiring more to get the same excitement. It is almost like a drug addiction, requiring constant increases in dosages to produce the same 'high'.

It then comes to pass that a peaceful house on a pleasant afternoon doesn't stimulate in the same way a new video game or toy will. The result is boredom. As David Wells has observed, good and evil have been collapsed into entertainment and boredom. The excitement of entertainment and activity is a far cry from what the Bible means by peace, our next fruit of the Spirit. Peace certainly can mean the absence of violence, and we will take note of today's violent influences a bit later when we consider gentleness. For now, we will focus on peace as intended in Galatians, a sense of completeness and wholeness stemming from proper relationships. We will first look more closely at some of the threats to such peace, and then we will consider the biblical teachings on the topic, contrast them with the threats, and finally consider practical suggestions for leading our children to savor peace in their lives.

Challenges to Our Children's Peace

We have just described a major threat to peace: the constant stimulation of postmodern life. We all experience this to some degree, such as when we can't drive without music playing, or cook dinner without a television on, or read a book for several hours without interrupting ourselves. We become restless, discontent unless we are entertained or active in some way, avoiding quietness and serenity like the plague. Most Christians sense that this is in some way wrong, but we don't quite understand how we became caught up in the whirlpool of stimulation.

There are even more insidious versions of this intensity of life for our children. Notice how schools are becoming more competitive, thus requiring more homework and effort so that even young children often feel immense pressure to perform in school. Once our children are home from school, what used to be called 'hobbies' are now more demanding than refreshing. If your child is on a sports team, practices may be long and frequent, with two or three games each week. Even individual activities require increasing time commitments, with music lessons requiring more hours and performances. Churches, too, speed up the whirlpool of life with more and more activities, including too many that separate family members from one another. The 'normal' Christian life is built around hurry, activity, and excessive stimulation. We are losing track of how to 'be still' and know who God is (Ps. 46: 10). The price of this is a shallowness of soul and relationships that leaves us afraid to be still lest we realize our sad estate. So long as we keep busy, maybe we can hide the poverty of our souls from ourselves. Sadly, our children pick up on this all too well.

Our children feel this stress themselves in many, many ways besides the school and play examples above. The new fad of teen blog sites means that to be 'cool' the teenager has to keep up with all the postings on the blogs of all their important friends. Children feel so much pressure to 'beat' video games (since friends have done so) that a large market has grown for providing 'cheat' codes. All of these speed the whirlpool even as our children don't realize what is happening. They become busier and busier, more and more stimulated, and think the solution to the unpleasant feelings that follow is to increase their speed even more. Yet, young minds need rest and relaxed, free, spontaneous play. Take, for example, the surprising advice of one sleep expert that teenagers need nine hours of sleep each night. I don't know about those you know, but this is far from the case for the young people I work with. 'You snooze, you lose' is more the motto of young people today. Little do they know the dangers of this as their parents think much the same way. Peace and quiet are not even virtues any more, equated as they are with boredom.

The effects of these attitudes include a sense of aimlessness and lack of direction. They feel more pulled than driven, just as in the whirlpool. Yet, a whirlpool eventually pulls things under the water, and this explains where the stress of modern life is taking our youth. Even young children are showing physical signs of stress and anxiety, with anxiety disorders being the most frequent psychological problems experienced by children. They develop eating and sleeping patterns that jeopardize their longevity, even as they learn from parents who do the same.

Such hurriedness and pressure reveals itself in other unpleasant emotions. What we call 'bored' is often irritation and thinly veiled anger at not being entertained or stimulated. Irritability is rampant among youngsters who want their way because they are so used to being stimulated in their favored fashion. If they are denied, anger follows. I wonder what percentage of confrontations parents have with their children is the direct result of denying their children some desired excitement. Watch children caught up in the intensity of a video game or competitive sporting event, and notice that what you see is not pleasure so much as anger and frustration. The promise of nonstop thrills in life doesn't deliver, yet our children and teenagers are powerfully drawn to this nonetheless.

And for what? There is little payoff, and this certainly doesn't fit the biblical description of the godly life. The hurried life merely distracts from the direction a Christian's life should be headed. It is even more dastardly in that the busyness itself discourages the self-reflection and quiet needed to see the problem in order to try to fix it. I sense the challenge of such stress as I battle it in my own life, even as I write these words. How can I teach children what I struggle so hard to conquer?

Such incessant activity also undermines relationships. Scurrying to and from football practice or ballet lessons is not what we would call quality time together. Watch a group of teenagers walking in the shopping mall. More will be conversing on cell phones than are interacting with the friends physically in the group. Families sit next to each other at home, but stare blankly at the television screen instead of talking to one another. Let us consider these relationships in more detail.

The stress and stimulation of modern life destroys the peer relationships of children and young people. They live to experience new thrills, and in the process, friendships are shorter lived. Even boy–girl relationships are not seen as romantic or deep, but are often simply one night stands where a couple 'hooks up' for a good time, eliciting memories of the words Tina Turner sang years ago, 'What's love got to do with it?' Notice how many of today's media are so individualized (Ipods, portable gaming devices, etc.) that they promote stimulation in isolation while discouraging friendships that meet deeper emotional and spiritual needs.

This trend also affects family relationships as each individual pursues his own excitement in his own technology. Dad watches the news on television while mum blogs on the Internet and the kids scurry to their video games and MP3 players. Once the excitement stops, notice how awkward simply being together becomes. You might try an experiment to check this out by having a one-evening fast from technology to simply be together, talk, or possibly play board games. This would remind you of what life could be outside the whirlpool...if we can adjust to it.

But no relationship is as adversely affected by such constant stimulation as one's relationship with God. As we already noted, if knowing God is promoted by being still, then we likely won't know God very well. How then will our children learn to hear the 'still small voice' of God through the blare of the latest tune on their Ipods? Even the thought of a 'quiet' time with God may threaten or at least bore our children. Notice how many youth ministers, instead of teaching young people a biblical way of life, exploit these trends to turn church youth activities into ever more stimulating events that perpetuate the whirlpool rather than showing a way out of it and into a walk with Christ.

Let's stop the action for a little while, pull back from our busyness and stress, and consider what the Bible teaches us about peace, for the sake of our children, ourselves and the kingdom of God.

The Bible on Peace

Most of us know the Hebrew word for peace, *shalom*, and that it serves as a greeting and parting blessing. It is seen in the Old Testament of course (e.g. Gen. 26: 29, 31; Exod. 4: 18; Judg. 18: 6; 2 Kgs 5: 19; 2 Sam. 15: 9), but people are often greeted or dismissed in peace in the New Testament as well (e.g. Luke 2: 29), with it being used at the beginning and the end of all the epistles except for James and 1 John. So what is this peace that forms such an integral part of our relating to one another in meeting and dismissing?

The focus of such peace is not so much the absence of overt warfare, but a state of soundness, wholeness and completeness,[2] with an implication of friendship, or peace in the relationship, when used as a greeting. Our modern usage captures the idea of soundness when we say things like 'I've come to peace with the loss' or 'I'm at peace about my decision.' As such, it refers to freedom from internal strife as opposed to freedom from external conflict as when peace is contrasted with war.

We quickly, then, see the problem with the intensity of life today: it makes for internal strife by not allowing opportunity to integrate the various aspects of our existence. This is an active process, as can be seen in what makes for a healthy marriage. The busy couple who scurry here and there without ever taking time to talk will not be seen as a couple that is close or lacking in strife. Staying so active that you can't see the areas of conflict is far different from being free of such conflict. A good relationship requires communication, personal growth, and give and take if it is to be free of strife and thus peaceful in this biblical sense.

The origin of personal peace is in God. To return to our whirlpool metaphor, we find peace moving in the stream of God's Word and will. When other concerns pull us away into the whirlpool, we stop flowing in God's will and begin the directionless circling that is faster and more stimulating, but at enmity with God. Thus, we must first see God as the source of peace, as recognized in the famous biblical blessing, 'The Lord bless you and keep you; the Lord make his face to shine upon you and be gracious to you; the Lord lift up his countenance upon you and give you peace' (Num. 6: 24–6). Eliphaz similarly diagnosed Job's distress as being due to disagreeing with God, and thus being deprived of God's peace (Job 22: 21). Peace could be simply defined as living a life in agreement with God's ways and will (Ps. 119: 165), with a lack of such peace showing where we disagree with God. This is why the wicked find no peace (Isa. 48: 22).

Peace also comes from knowing God's protection and trusting in him, as stated in the wonderful text of Isaiah 26: 3, 'You keep him in perfect peace whose mind is stayed on you, because he trusts in you.' Such trust even leads to peaceful sleep (Ps. 4: 8). Often peace is thus offered as the antidote to fear (Gen. 43: 23; Judges 6: 23) with prayer in particular being the avenue to finding such peace (Phil. 4: 7). Of particular consolation is the covenant promise of God to teach our children so that they will know great peace (Isa. 54: 13).

The prospect of peace with God, with ourselves, and with others is rooted in the Prince of Peace (Isa. 9: 6). Basic to Christian theology is the problem of our sin alienating us from God. A holy God cannot fellowship with sin, yet it taints all of us. The Trinity, in incomprehensible love, solves the problem as the Father sends the Son to die for our sins so the Father can adopt us as children and grant us peace with him. Paul develops this breathtaking truth in Romans, culminating in 5: 1 where we learn our justification works our peace with God, freeing us to leave our sinful striving against God. The Old Testament peace offerings (e.g. Exod. 32: 6; Lev. 3, 7) show this, as part of the animal sacrificed to God is eaten by the person, showing a communion with God made possible by forgiveness and peace restored. This image deepens the meaning of the sacrament of communion as we share a meal with Jesus, who sacrificed himself for our sin so we might be at peace with the Father.

Still we stray and sacrifice this peace in our day-to-day lives, and in so doing lead our children away from the precious peace of God as we are sucked into the whirlpool of worldly stimulation and distraction. Let us see how we can use these truths to draw our lives and those of our little ones out of the irritating and ceaseless swirl and into the stream of God's peace.

God's Peace Versus Stimulating Strivings

Let's first consider God's economy of time. In a day where efficiency is king, we seek to do as much as we can as fast as we can. If I think in terms of efficiency, God isn't very good. Take Moses as an example. If he had become leader of the children of Israel earlier, they could have been freed sooner and suffered less. Yet God ripens his servant for ministry through long years away (Exod. 2.11–4: 31). Jesus himself spent three years of his thirty-three years of life in public ministry. That's something like nine per cent of his time in human flesh. I would have come up with a 'better' plan so he accomplished 'more' while here. We sometimes live as though God hasn't laid down his plan well enough and we have to push and hurry to get things done for God. We forget the pacing of Jesus' life in particular, where he would come aside for prayer and never seemed in too big of a hurry to bless a child or turn to someone in need. Why would we think God would want our lives to be so intense that we cannot even mirror the life of our Lord and Savior? It is because we want to produce and be active rather than believe God at work within us. Our children learn from and copy us unless we point them away from the whirlpool and to the 'still waters' offered by the Good Shepherd of Psalm 23.

If we will stop and be still, we will know that God's love for us is unconditional and that striving to do things on our own is not his way. We must make this change and teach our children through our example and our words. We must restrain them from the whirlpool that is swirling all around.

I am moved by the title of Søren Kierkegaard's book, *Purity of Heart is to Will One Thing*. Here is the ceasing of internal conflicts as our wills are fully aligned with God's. One of the most exciting prospects of heaven is that I will no longer even be tempted by sin as I am freed from this duplicity in my life. I thus want to follow Christ and not be distracted or double-minded by seeking the fleeting thrills of the whirlpool of life. Our children, too, will find peace within themselves only when they are unified in heart to follow Christ. This doesn't require of us money or programs or formal activities. It is the fruit of prayer, example, and parental discipline. We must show our little ones that peace is a wonderful virtue, and that it is not found in a hectic pace of life or the love of worldly stimulations.

We cannot have stronger relationships in our lives, and the lives of our children, until we slow down and do the things that make for peace. Parents need to spend more time alone talking to each other, discussing their mission as parents and praying for their children. This is where we learn to trust God for our children's spiritual well-being and not become trapped into thinking our busyness will accomplish this. As we noted at the beginning, the fruit of the Spirit is just that—given by the Spirit. While we seek to avoid distractions from the Spirit's work, we must remember he is more concerned about our children than we are. Pausing to consider this brings great peace.

We also need to build peace in our relationship with our children. We are so goal-focused sometimes that we do not

93

make peaceful moments together. Stop the action and go for a walk (without Ipods or cell phones). Have a picnic. Sit outdoors and look at the stars. Teach your children the joys of being at peace by engaging them in peace-giving activities. How much stronger will relationships grow under the stars than watching the stars on television!

We must show our children how to have friendships that are peace-full. Teach them the advantages of truly communicating with their friends apart from the frenzy of technology. I was delighted when our daughter wanted to celebrate her sixteenth birthday by having friends over to play boards games where they talked to each other and enjoyed each other's company in person. If we guide them in this long enough, they will see the peace of good relationships in contrast to the frenzied stimulation of shallow relationships.

Our churches should afford our children and young people alternatives to the chaos of life, not try to imitate it in our programs. Youth programs that try to look like the culture miss the fact that the culture is not peace-giving. Teenagers should be together to fellowship in Christ, building relationships through fun activities for sure, but also by praying for one another, helping others in need, and cultivating an inner sense of integrity around their identity as followers of Christ.

We see then how we must abandon the ever-accelerating pace of modern life and live an alternative way that shows we trust God to provide and to teach our children that peace is preferable to pace. We must show them the simple joys of nature and of simplicity of heart in following Christ. We must cultivate relationships with our children that promote peace between them and us, especially as one of the best safeguards against sinful behavior in adolescence is the young person's desire to protect the peace and trust in her relationship with her parents. Once again, the key to providing a context for the fruit of peace is in offering a different culture to our families and in our churches.

Practical Steps toward Lives of Peace

We have considered lofty aims in this chapter, and these may intimidate us rather than challenge us. Let us, then, finish this discussion with some practical steps of progress in peace rather than assuming we will be perfect in the task.

PRESCHOOL CHILDREN

E stablish a routine 'peaceful' time each day, such as reading a book together, taking a walk, etc.

Teach creative ways to play by avoiding toys related to television shows, movies, etc. A sand box is one suggestion as it is quiet, creative, and allows interaction.

Similarly, limit television, movies, and video games. This is the age where you can avoid the whirlpool rather than introducing your children to it.

When doing something peaceful, deliberately state to your child(ren) how peaceful it is so they learn to recognize and appreciate such activities.

Make church nurseries and preschool programs environments of peace. Use them to build relationships between church members and children, and minimize highly stimulating media.

ELEMENTARY SCHOOL CHILDREN

E stablish a 'quiet hour' or more each day where no media is used or music playing (unless it is played on instruments by you or your children).

Resist activities that speed up the pace of life excessively.

Make meal times quiet by sitting at the table, turning off background noises such as televisions and telephones. Linger after dinner to talk, have a devotional time, or play a game.

Continue teaching the dangers of media addiction and stimulation, deliberately (yes, I'm using that word often!) teaching them the lifestyles of the heroes of the Bible in contrast to contemporary ways of living.

In church Sunday Schools and activities, don't underestimate the power of storytelling from the Bible and from the lives of Christian leaders and missionaries. Don't concede Christian education to high-powered and intense strategies, trusting God to work in the faithful proclamation of his Word.

TEENAGERS

Set limits on Internet, video game, television, and cell phone time while encouraging activities that build peace-full friendships such as having friends over to visit.

Teaching your child now is less didactic and more Socratic. That is, it involves more questioning than dictating. Listen and lead by questions so your teen feels comfortable in talking with you and thus peace is maintained in your relationship.

Guide your teenager to resources and habits that promote an open, peaceful relationship with God. Don't underestimate the types of Christian books they can grasp, and encourage time alone with God in peace. Teach them to will one thing as you address the problems of growing up.

Plan longer family times of peace. Vacation for a weekend in the mountains and enjoy nature rather than at the active spots with lots of people, noise, and whirlpools.

Encourage youth programs at church that promote peace. These will afford time for the youth to build relationships with one another under godly guidance, and will include interactions with the other generations at the church. Fun activities are balanced with ones that promote reflection and peace with God.

7

'I WANT PATIENCE AND I WANT IT NOW!'

Maria was tiring of the pressure. She had been going out with
Patrick for several weeks now, and he had made it clear that
his professed Christian faith did not hinder him from wanting
to have sex with her. As if that were not enough, her friends
knew what was going on and hounded her at school to learn
if she had 'done it' yet. Maria's talk of waiting until marriage
did nothing to slow the pressure from Patrick and her friends.
'It's fun.' 'Why wait? It won't hurt anything.' 'You won't get
pregnant.' 'It's natural when you love someone.' 'What are you
waiting for? No one stays a virgin anymore.' Maria found being
patient to be hard work. Not much in her life had prepared her
to take this stand, and she wondered how she could hold out for
the several years before marriage would be a realistic option.

Maria's challenge exemplifies the many similar dilemmas
faced by today's youth. Raised on a steady diet of instant
gratification, they are grievously unprepared to say 'no' when
resisting temptation or waiting for something better to come
along. The cultural trends we examined in our discussion of
peace have ramifications for the grace of patience as well. We
have become accustomed to immediate satisfaction of so many
of our desires that we have lost the virtue of patience. Let us

consider ways life today promotes impatience before we turn again to God's Word for guidance in remediating this plague and wisdom in raising children who know how to wait and thus can stand in the day of temptation.

Paths to Impatience

I remember hearing someone say he knew he lived in a modern age when he found himself becoming impatient while waiting on the microwave oven. I remember growing up, my father would get a pan, pour in some oil and we'd wait a while for it to heat, then we'd add popcorn, and in a few minutes we'd have a tasty snack (followed by some cleaning up). Today, zip the prepackaged popcorn in the microwave and in a couple of minutes you have hot, pre-seasoned popcorn in a ready-to-eat container that you simply toss in the trash when you're finished. This is but an example of our instant society where we come to believe patience is no longer needed. Let's examine this more closely.

First, consider the change in movie viewing. Years ago you waited all week, if not for weeks at a time, for a chance to see a movie on the weekend. It was a social event to be enjoyed with friends. Now we have personal copies of more movies than I even saw in my childhood, all seconds away from entertaining us in our DVD players. No longer a social event most times, movies are now instant enjoyment. No queuing for tickets, no waiting in line for refreshments (remember our microwave popcorn?), and no matching schedules to plan a time.

Children now have television programming designed for them available constantly. The Saturday morning cartoon hours have given way to twenty-four hour cartoon channels. If a child doesn't like what's on, she has dozens of DVDs to choose from and likely her own DVD player and television in her own room. No need to wait your turn for the family set when you have your own. A child no longer needs to trek to the local library to do research for school. A few clicks on the Internet and one has more resources than can be used. Cell phones mean you can reach most anyone instantly, no matter where they may be (even in public restrooms, I've learned to my disdain). Email makes communicating with people far away instantaneous, making 'snail mail' obsolete in most cases.

Does your little one have a headache? There's a children's painkiller ready to take away the suffering, no matter how slight. Does he want something in the store? Even if you lack cash, you can make him happy (not joyful!) still by pulling out your trusty credit card. Is Sally hungry? Quick snacks are always available to satisfy any peckish whim. See something you like on the Shopping Channel, 'call now' is the plea as your credit card again makes impulse shopping border on an addiction. Modern technology has made for instant everything it seems, and for the most part we are grateful for these conveniences that do indeed make life easier.

But just as all medicines have side effects, so do modern conveniences. The more we become accustomed to having so many wishes granted in a hurry, the more we come to expect that in every thing. Yet, this simply isn't true. Though travel is faster today, more cars make for traffic jams. Traffic jams lead to road rage for those who forget that everything is instant. We need to consider the dangers of an instant society as it is a breeding ground for impatience.

I hinted at some of the dangers of instant gratification in my earlier examples. Making popcorn with my father was a special time when we did this together. The efficiency of microwave popcorn comes at the expense of some of the good times parents and children share when they prepare foods together. Even the convenience of owning DVDs costs some of the community pleasures of a night out at the movies. This is often a relational price we pay for instant gratification.

But the most dangerous side effect of getting our way so frequently is the sense of entitlement it begets, particularly in our children. There has been great cultural pressure in recent years to build our children's self-esteem as that was seen as the secret to success for our children in every arena. Christian parents bought into the idea since it came not only from secular sources, but from trusted Christian authorities as well. Part of this shallow notion of self-esteem is that any disappointment or frustrated desire would harm the child's feelings about herself, resulting in problems ranging from poor grades to poor friendships to depression to alcoholism. So, many Christian parents scrambled to give their children every opportunity to feel good about themselves. They satisfied whims, bought tons of toys and gadgets, affirmed any effort at academics or sports, even praising effort when answers were blatantly wrong. Parents gave children lots of choices in areas like what's for dinner, where to go this weekend, when to take a bath or go to bed, which clothes to wear, when to get ears pierced or wear makeup, when to come home, and so on. This conveniently served the dual purpose of appeasing many parents of the guilt they felt for spending so little time with their children.

But what does this accomplish? Subsequent research has proven this advice to be disastrous. Jean Twenge has depicted this in detail in her *Generation Me*[1] but here we will focus on the impact of this on Christian families in particular. Parents who profess Christ are generally stronger disciplinarians than others, and have still done a good job of punishing misbehaviors. But giving so many choices and affirmations apart from their being earned deprives children of the opportunity to develop character—which includes patience. Constantly asking little children to choose creates additional stress in their lives, conflicting with peace, but it also leaves them feeling they can have whatever they want whenever they want it. As Twenge notes, this doesn't produce self-esteem, but a dangerous form of selfishness called narcissism. These children become little astronomers, believing the world revolves around them since they are the center of the universe. Combine this with the instant satisfactions of technology, and you have a generation of children who not only expect to get what they want, but to get it instantly. Gone is the virtue of persevering toward a goal by persisting in hardship and overcoming adversity. Instant gratification is the key. Adults grant success with no expectation that effort and energy are required by the child to achieve it. Here is a perfect recipe for impatience. If young Maria never had to wait to get the dinner she wanted, or to wear the clothes she liked, or to study hard to make good grades, then what in her life has prepared her to wait to have sex with her boyfriend? Or how will any of these children grow to learn to sustain effort toward larger goals such as college degrees or staying in careers? More importantly, how will they garner the character to persevere in a marital relationship with its ups and downs, or in parenting children who require huge amounts of patience? But most importantly, how will this produce children who share in God's perfectly patient character?

If we move past the notion of patience to the older term of longsuffering, how will we teach children in this age to suffer long if they never suffer 'short', or are never even taught that there can be benefit in suffering at all? We need to reflect on the teachings of Scripture on the matter so that we can change the ways we are training impatience to match the ways of our Heavenly Father in teaching patience to his children.

Patience in Scripture

Patience is a virtue simply because it is rooted in the character of God (Rom. 2: 4; 9: 22) and thus of his Son (1 Tim. 1: 16). Just as simply, then, to be impatient is to be ungodly in our character and behavior. God's patience can be seen as a function of his other perfections. If he is sovereign, all-powerful, all-knowing, and fully in control of all things, his timing is never frustrated and he accomplishes his purposes in their proper time. Our impatience results from our wanting such a degree of control in our lives for our purposes. We want people to do as we say and when we say it. We want our desires gratified immediately. Conversely, patience is when we rest in the sovereignty of God to know he will do what is right in his time.

Our patience comes from knowing God will keep his promises to us (2 Tim. 4: 2, 8; Heb. 6: 12). Trusting God's timing yields patience in hearing and keeping the Word as we await its fruit (Luke 8: 15). We are commanded to be patient (Titus 2: 2) by imitating those who were faithful and patient in awaiting their inheritance of God's promises (Heb. 6: 12).

The call to patience is seen in the Old Testament especially in the common refrain to wait for the Lord. Psalm 37: 7 encourages us not to lose heart when the wicked prosper, but to rest in God and wait patiently for him. The Psalms are filled with examples of this call to wait and of believers embodying it (Ps. 25: 3; 27: 14; 33: 20; 37: 34; 62: 5; 130: 5). It is those who wait on the Lord who will inherit the earth (Ps. 37: 9) and are blessed (Isa. 30: 18). One of the most famous texts on the topic is Isaiah 40: 31, which teaches us that 'they who wait for the Lord shall renew their strength; they shall mount up with wings like eagles; they shall run and not be weary; they shall walk and not faint.'

Implicit in this theme of Scripture is that we will experience times when it seems God is far from us and when things we long for—even good things like the victory of good over evil— appear impossible. The believer's response is to remind himself that God is not in a hurry and will accomplish his purposes in his time. Patience is tolerating adversity and frustration because we trust in the God who is in control of all things.

This, of course, is more easily said than done. Remember the Bible was written long before all the modern conveniences we have discussed in this chapter, so we are far more accustomed to getting things quickly and thus far less inclined to wait. Even as I write this on my computer, I fight the urge to check my email, to look at sports scores, or scan news headlines. How are we to learn patience for ourselves, much less teach it to our children?

Making a Place for Patience

The key text in applying the biblical teachings to our topic is James 1: 2–4: 'Count it all joy, my brothers, when you meet trials of various kinds, for you know that the testing of your faith produces steadfastness. And let steadfastness have its full effect, that you may be perfect and complete, lacking in nothing.' The King James Version translates 'steadfastness' as 'patience', though the similarity of the terms is obvious. The first point here is the assumption that the reader will experience various trials, and trials most certainly include frustrations and delayed gratifications. We need then to admit that tough times will come for everyone. Modern life cannot deliver on its promise of freedom from suffering and frustration. We must also make this clear to our children.

We also see that patience comes in the testing of one's faith, another assumption James makes regarding his readers. The tongue-in-cheek title of this chapter captures the illogical reasoning we often live by: we want to be patient, but want it to be injected into us like a medicine, not have it forged in the fires of adversity. As parents and those who minister to children, we must forsake the doctrines of self-esteem, and reorient our efforts to coincide with God's Word by seeing hardships as important learning experiences, not hindrances to self-worth. It seems the idea of protecting children from adversity was precisely backwards. It is much like the idea of immunization: if we are not exposed to germs at all, our bodies cannot develop the antibodies needed to combat them. So with frustrations: our children cannot be patient in hardship if they have no training in coping with tough circumstances. Our children can't be 'long-suffering' if we try to avoid all suffering.

Finally, our text makes clear that our attitude about trials is not merely one of expectation and endurance, but one of embracing them. We are to take joy in the difficulties of life. I imagine a tennis player who only plays easy opponents and never loses a match. Such a player will never play on the revered courts at Wimbledon. A player needs to be challenged to improve, and so welcomes opponents that build skill. So it is in learning patience, and teaching it to our children.

This means, then, that those of us who care for our children and those of our churches, should actually encourage enduring hardships in life, not seek to protect our children from all of them. Obviously this does not imply that we are deliberately to make them suffer, or to be indifferent to serious suffering or dangers faced by our children. It does suggest, however, that we need to be a bit less protective of them. We should let them sweat through challenging school assignments rather than do the work for them. We should choose the clothing for little children, at least most of the time, simply so they learn that their wants are not the engine that drives their lives. We need to be firm in discipline, fulfilling consequences we promise so our children learn our word is true and that mistakes bring consequences. As I often advise parents, we are preparing children for a world where teachers, friends, employers, or spouses won't coddle them the way we do. So it is better to learn difficult lessons from loving parents than to be insulated and then thrown to the real world. We want to parent in a way that prepares our Marias for the challenge of being patient.

More than this, however, we want our children to be patient in spiritual matters, for this is the clear thrust of the texts we have considered. Foundational to this is our need to teach our children of God's sovereignty. This is a day when various ideas about God are floating around, most of which deprive him of the glory he deserves for his greatness. A series of family devotionals around the doctrine of God's sovereignty might be a place to begin this process. Sunday School teachers also might teach on God's providence to reinforce to our children that God is in control, and will work things out in his way and in his timing. They need merely to wait patiently for him.

But just knowing God's providence as a theological concept is not to live in light of it. Parents do well to help their children see God's actions in all of life. When a child is struggling in school, point her to God's comfort in this time of suffering and to the wonderful ways he will eventually work this to his glory. Whatever the circumstance our children encounter, parents will teach their children to wait on the sovereign Lord. The biblical story of Joseph is most suitable to making this point as we remind ourselves and our children that though the circumstances seem dark, God still intends it to us for good.

There is one other vital gift from God that promotes patience, and that is the gift of Sabbath rest. American Christians in particular are amusing, for we fight to have the Ten Commandments posted in government offices, but live as though one of them is irrelevant. Yet the Sabbath principle remains, though we now celebrate it on the first day of the week to honor Jesus' resurrection. It is easy to believe our children need to practice their sports or musical instruments, or to work on homework projects for school, or keep pushing on in other ways. This defeats our pursuit of peace as we discussed in our last chapter, but I mention it here because it also sabotages patience as we assume our busyness cannot wait until Monday. Dedicating the day to worship, focusing our hearts on our Savior, and enjoying family and church relationships all promote spiritual well-being for us and our children. Most who choose to keep the Sabbath find enough time and energy to complete their work responsibilities in six days, and learn the joy of knowing they can be patient about getting it done.[2]

We end this chapter with a reminder that there is no formula for any of the Spirit's fruit. Patience is a gift from God and not something we 'accomplish' by doing certain things. We set out in this study to demonstrate the insidious ways that living in the twenty-first century contradict and threaten fruit in the lives of our children. We have seen in this chapter how immediate gratification and never having to wait work against patience in the lives of our children, rendering them weak against the times when waiting is called for. All of our children will face situations like Maria's in some respect, and we want to prepare them with Christian thinking and practice so that the grace of patience will find a welcome home in their lives. Let us ask God for patience with us, for us to be patient with our children, and for them to know the joy of the fruit of longsuffering.

Patient Steps

In considering ways to promote patience in our children, it is probably wise to bear in mind that such a quality will not come quickly, and we do well to demonstrate it even as we try to teach it.

PRESCHOOL CHILDREN

Prevention is easier than cure, so prayerfully consider your philosophy of parenting to see where you can allow your child to experience and learn from minor frustrations.

One simple example is to limit the child's food choices for meals, or even better, let him know he can choose the dinner menu on Saturday if he does not complain about the menu during the week. Once limited, choices can be effective rewards.

Deliberately use the term 'patient' with children. For instance, when waiting for a turn in the bathroom, say 'This is a good time to show how you can be patient.'

Teach stories from the Bible that focus on God's providence and the patience of his people.

Of course, children learn by watching, so seek God for patience in front of your little ones. This may be especially important at church, and how patient you and others are toward children.

ELEMENTARY SCHOOL AGES

L imit access to entertainment activities until chores and homework are done, teaching children to be patient for the 'fun' until responsibilities are complete.

Avoid buying things that they want on a whim. Have them save money for those things, and have them earn the funds by working. They learn more of your love by your teaching them to patiently work for things than by your just giving them what they want.

Add the terms 'providence' and 'sovereignty' to their vocabularies as you teach them why it is good to wait for the Lord

Reward patience. Let your child know when she has been patient, say so, and even surprise her with an occasional treat for so doing.

Churches can help teach children patience by having them spend time with groups of older persons in the congregation. For example, children can serve a meal to seniors.

TEENAGERS

T he principle of freedom and responsibility is vital in the adolescent years. Don't just give privileges, but have your teen earn them by demonstrating an appropriate responsibility. For example, don't just grant a later curfew, but offer to lengthen it by thirty minutes when the old one is kept faithfully and without complaint for a set period of time.

Teaching is better done via questions with teens in many ways. Question them as to why waiting for certain things is preferable. These range from sex to driving, drinking, dating, and getting married. Ask them to think about how God's providence plays a role in their reasoning.

By now your children should have more choices, but the privilege of choosing should come from patient acceptance of times when they can't have their way. Make this relationship clear to them.

There are many relationship struggles as friends are vital to teenagers. Encourage them to communicate this, and guide them to seeing that the suffering they experience is a path to growth and patience.

Where better to learn patience than in interactions with others who might test it. Actively involve teenagers in church activities where they must deal with other people. Have them usher people into worship services, or plan activities together so they learn the patience of working as a team.

8

DELIBERATE ACTS OF KINDNESS

The phone rings, and the caller informs Martha of the mischief done to her son by Martha's son as he put cheese whiz in his shoes at school that day. Martha reacts with a thinly veiled smile at the cleverness of the misdeed while saying her son will apologize. Such are the mixed messages our children receive from the media about naughty deeds. In this case, taken from a popular family comedy program, by the end of the show, the mother understands her son's behavior to be justifiable because she experiences how annoying the victim is when she spends some time with him. We are unmistakably left to think a clever, 'harmless' prank is fine, especially if it is done to someone we don't particularly like.

An entire book could be written describing the way the media portrays meanness as funny. The generally innocent mishaps of 'Leave It to Beaver' have evolved into the deliberate naughtiness of Bart Simpson. On closer inspection, even older cartoons played mean-spiritedness for a laugh. I was particularly impressed with how mean the animated Jerry was to Tom—going far beyond what was needed to ensure his own safety to inflict considerable harm on the celebrated cat. Yet it is true in this case that 'art imitates life' as children are indeed mean to one another. Since usually no one is hurt badly, we adults may not take this too seriously or may give off our own mixed messages about the prank being wrong although a 'good one'.

The most common excuse for letting unkind acts be is that 'boys will be boys', as though simply the maleness makes these actions morally acceptable. But we cannot exempt girls here either. Angelique, of the famed cartoon 'Rugrats' is no little lady, for example. We are being trained to view meanness as a way to get a good laugh, seeing it as only natural and thus not in need of change or challenge.

Life mirrors the media portrayal. Boys fight and do naughty things. Girls have developed their own special brand of sophisticated meanness whereby they hurt each other emotionally in clever ways, playing especially on the insecurities of early adolescence. This has led to a small library of books addressing the new ways that females fight.

While we might have our opinions, we easily slip from constructive criticism to personal derision. Many Christian families tolerate subtle forms of meanness as we speak negatively of others in our conversations. Some of this our children learn from adults as we, for instance, dissect the pastor and his sermon as we drive home from church, or else we speak disparagingly of Ms. Smith's tacky outfit or Mr. Jones' inane idea for improving the church parking lot.

Acts of unkindness are legion in our time, and most go unnoticed and thus are implicitly accepted. Yet, even if we were to eliminate these, it is a far cry from doing good. Being kind is a much loftier ambition than simply not being unkind. Peter Gourevitch chronicled the genocide in Rwanda and lamented how the world sat passively by as 800,000 people were brutally slain, even though the acts were denounced. His conclusion? 'To denounce evil is a far cry from doing good.'

Our world encourages cruelty, oppression, and other forms of disregard for our fellow humans. Yet against this stands the Spirit's medicinal fruit of kindness. Why is it so common to mistreat others, and how are we to protect our children from these trends and to promote kindness in its stead? This chapter seeks to offer some answers to these important questions.

How Not to Be Kind

Kindness, of course, has never come too easily to most folks. Selfishness comes pretty naturally to toddlers; it is sharing that has to be taught...and retaught. This is readily explained by the biblical doctrine of original sin which teaches that we sin because we are born with sinful natures. As I explained in *Of Such is the Kingdom*, the sin problem is the reason parents have to discipline and instruct children in the first place. It causes a naturally drift to serve self rather than God or others, as seen in the first sin in the Garden of Eden. Yet our day is coming up with new ways to worsen an old problem.

Self-centeredness is the crux of the problem. Though it has always been with us, most cultures have at least made some effort to restrain it and to proclaim the value of service to others. Psychology, sociology, and economics have converged to put self on the throne as it never was before.

Psychology is the source of the focus on the self-esteem we have already discussed. It explained to us that we must feel good about ourselves to be healthy and happy. It spread to every corner of Western culture and permeates our educational systems, though gratefully its proponents are starting to see its problems. Yet this means people spend their lives pursuing the elusive commodity of self-esteem, leaving them self-absorbed and largely oblivious to others. This even shockingly entered the Christian community through a scandalous interpretation of Jesus' words in the Great Commandment (Matt. 22: 39; Mark 12: 31; Luke 10: 27). This view holds that, if we are to love our neighbors as ourselves, we must first come to love ourselves. That is, until we have a high level of self-esteem, we are incapable of loving others (and thus relieved of responsibility for failing to do so). Such a treatment of the text sorely misunderstands Jesus who rightly assumes we love ourselves adequately if not excessively. This view made actively seeking to love oneself no longer selfish, but an act of obedience to Jesus. Though not as explicit, note how much current Christian literature focuses on self and how faith is therapeutic.

The philosophy of self-esteem coincided with the sixties cultural revolution and its freeing us from institutions and rules. Though initially this was built on values of loving one another, this ideology quickly fell prey to selfism and merely gave us increased right to please ourselves.

A society of free, anti-authoritarian individuals out there is the marketer's dream come true. Whether as partial cause or simply an effect, the advertising industry fueled the frenzy of self. We learned we needed more and more products not to meet basic needs, but to meet psychological ones. In short, we were told the road to self-esteem was more stuff. If we wanted our children to feel good about themselves (the goal of the majority of parents), there were thousands of products to make it happen. McDonald's told us we deserve a break today, and others told us we were worth the indulgence of the product.

We see this in the competitiveness of sports as winning is everything, because life has no place for 'losers'. I still recall my daughter playing soccer at age six when officially the teams were not even supposed to keep score. One game, our happy-go-lucky players looked to the other end of the field to see their opponents warming up only to shudder when they saw with each practice shot their coach yelled to them, 'Kill!' a bit much for six-year-olds, don't you think? (And yes, we lost that match!) Immense rivalries develop between children and groups of children. As they grow, they compete to garner self-esteem at any cost.

The softer side of this is also noted in the advertising we mentioned. Once away from competition, life is about doing what you like and enjoying leisure. You deserve such treatment, whether it be a vacation in the Caribbean, or a posh meal at an expensive restaurant, or more comfortable lounge chair for viewing television.

And so life becomes a frenzied pursuit of self. One time-honored way to feel better about your self, as we know, is to put another person down. If you are a dummy, or a nerd, or a misfit of some type, then I must be okay because at least I'm better than you. How many of us have seen this type of reasoning in the lives of our children (and of ourselves!)? Being unkind is a backwards way of trying to feel good about oneself, while at the same time it flows from not feeling good about oneself because of one's sin (whether we realize this part or not).

This is not a world that encourages kindness, where we go out of our way to help another person. This is a world where doing good to another may take something away from our self and give that person some advantage. Moreover, it is a world where, even for those who value kindness, the passionate pursuit of self-gratification blinds us to opportunities for kindness.

This is the central area of concern for Christian parents. It's relatively easy to correct our children for unkind deeds, but it is a challenge to open their eyes to how much kindness is needed in our world. Psychology tells us the first step to behaving morally is to recognize situations with a moral need. When our children are absorbed in themselves, they see only what will help them and relegate the needs of others to the periphery of their perception. We as parents and those who care for children may inadvertently contribute to this as we are caught in the pursuit of self-esteem and self-satisfaction. We may stop bad behaviors, but we must intentionally cultivate acts of kindness in our children.

As we live in our cozy suburban homes and go to our comfortable and secure churches, we have little need to see the squalor of the world. If we don't notice the moral urgency of the world, we will never act in kindness toward it. Consider that our children spend 16–17 hours a week on the Internet or email but only about 3 hours helping others in some capacity. That's not even to mention the countless hours of television.

Yet, almost one billion people in the world get too little food each day[1], and several billion more have diets that are poor in necessary nutrients, even as 600 million people are overnourished and overweight (mostly in North America and Europe). In developing countries, six million children die each year, largely due to malnourishment. Yet the basic health and nutrition needs of the world's poorest people could be met for about $13 billion more a year. Listen closely: Americans and Europeans spend more than that each year on pet food! Since we don't usually see these people, we fail to act in kindness as we miss the moral imperative of their situation.

We could talk of needs closer to home as people suffer in loneliness in nursing homes, smile at church while their families are falling apart at home, and live lives of suffering and pain in our neighborhoods. We want to be followers of Christ who indeed love these neighbors as ourselves, and who guide our children to doing the same. Let us then consider what the Bible has to say on kindness to equip us for this work.

Loving Kindness

If our children are to love kindness, we must help them understand it in all its beauty. We are to be kind because God himself is kind in all his works (Ps. 145: 17). He leads his people with kindness (Hos. 11: 4), with repentance being our appropriate response (Rom. 2: 4). Stop for a moment to consider this. Repentance comes from our grasping and properly appreciating God's kindness to us. Here is our first teaching point for our children: we are to point out to them God's many kindnesses toward them. What are kindnesses? There is no deep meaning to the biblical terms: they are simply acts of good favor toward others. That we are breathing, have eyes to see these words and mind enough to understand them— these are samples of God's kindnesses toward us.

Jesus as the Son of God lived a life of kindness among us as he reached out repeatedly to the undeserving (examples include Mark 10: 13–16; Luke 7: 11–17, 36–50; 8: 40–56; 13: 10–17; 18: 15–17, 27: 26; John 8: 1–11; 19: 25–7). In contrast to the interpretation we discussed above, Jesus' Great Commandment calls us to love our neighbor as ourselves, and this will be seen in acts of kindness reflecting our Savior's own loving kindness.

Scripture is full of examples of kindness. Many times kindness is shown merely in the way one speaks to another, as when the king of Babylon spoke kindly to Jehoiachin and let him out of prison (Jer. 52: 32). At other times kindness is due in response to receiving it. Joseph (Gen. 40: 14) asks the cupbearer to show him the kindness of mentioning him to Pharaoh in response to Joseph's kindness in interpreting his dream. In 1 Samuel 15: 6, the Kenites are shown kindness because they showed mercy to the children of Israel, and in 2 Samuel 9: 1 David shows kindness to Mephibosheth for the sake of Jonathan. Joash is viewed negatively when he does not return an act of kindness (2 Chr. 24: 22).

Often acts of kindness are spontaneous, including the angels helping Lot escape Sodom (Gen. 19: 19). Notably, the natives of Malta showed 'unusual kindness' to Paul by welcoming them and building a fire to warm him and his companions (Acts 28: 2). Yet kindnesses can be in response to a request, such as Peter's responding to Cornelius' request in Acts 10: 33, or Paul asking Felix to hear him. Even being rebuked by a righteous man is a kindness according to Psalm 141: 5. The wicked man is denounced by David, 'For he did not remember to show kindness, but pursued the poor and needy and the brokenhearted, to put them to death' (Ps. 109: 16). This verse is convicting as it directly associates helping the financially or even emotionally burdened with being kind. The wealthy Western church stands rebuked on this account, I'm afraid, and I number myself among the transgressors who fail to show kindness to these people.

Kindness is expected, and thus it is commanded. Paul commands the Ephesians to be kind, tenderhearted, and forgiving (4: 32). The oft-quoted text of Micah 6: 8 confirms this, 'he has told you, O man, what is good; and what does the Lord require of you but to do justice, and to love kindness, and to walk humbly with your God.' Once more kindness is tied to treating the poor and others justly. Proverbs (11: 17; 21: 21) advises us that there are personal benefits to being kind. Naomi sees Boaz's kindness to Ruth as being an act of God's kindness as well (Ruth 2: 13, 20), showing how we are God's instruments when we are kind.

Most of the acts described in Scripture depict men in acts of kindness, but there is a special value of the gentle deeds of women. Proverbs 31 is the familiar depiction of the godly woman, and verse 26 notes that such a woman teaches kindness. Here is a clear call to mothers in particular. Titus 2: 5 reinforces this as it stresses that women in particular are to be kind.

Two places that flesh out what kindness looks like merit special attention. The first is the 'Golden Rule' of Luke 6: 31, 'As you wish that others would do to you, do so to them.' This text offers a plain guide to being kind: put yourself in the shoes of the other person, and do for them what you would want done to you. Notice this is a deliberate action, and acts of kindness are unlikely if we don't take the time to stop and see the other's perspective. Children will learn this from us as they see us do it in our daily lives.

The other place I would mention is Jesus' parable of the Good Samaritan (Luke 10: 25–37) where our Lord teaches us who our neighbor is. It is hard enough to be kind to friends and family, but our neighbor includes everyone. We are called to go out of our way to show mercy and grace to those we may not even like, for this is where we truly act like Jesus.

Our survey shows that the simple idea of being kind to one another is more demanding than we might have thought, even without the societal hindrances we discussed above. How are we to raise children who are kind like their Lord?

Moving Toward Kindness

It is obvious that creating a child with a kind heart is not a three easy step process. Kindness is forged in the grind of our daily existence and, to remind ourselves yet again, it is ultimately a fruit of the Holy Spirit. With these caveats in mind, I venture to offer a few steps that may help.

First, as those who care for children, we need to expose the unkindnesses of the world for what they are. We must confront mean-spirited behavior in our children, punishing it as it deserves. We cannot excuse boys just being boys, but we must keep focused on our calling to raise our children in the ways of the Lord. When we see naughty behavior in the media, don't let it pass but bring it to our young ones' attention so they learn to take notice and not be blinded by casual familiarity with meanness. Such challenges will likely be in the form of questions when addressing older children, such as 'Though that may seem funny, can you think of a more Christlike way to have handled this?'

Then, remember your goals as parents. You are raising children who believe in Christ and hunger and thirst after righteousness. This is not the same as having self-esteem as a goal. You will have to cope with being different from many of the parents around you, but we are to do right, not what is popular. Remember the great reformer John Calvin saw self-denial as the key to the Christian life, a stark contrast to the self-esteem teachings of our day. Is this a morbid way of life? To the contrary, in denying our self-interest, we are freed to enjoy the things of God. As we saw in discussing joy, this is where we find true happiness anyway. Make your goals evident to your children regularly and do not be shy to point out how this is different from the philosophies of the world around them. Comment on the lies of advertising, challenge the messages of media, alert them to rude behaviors in public places, and question school policies that miss the mark.

Become more aware of God's kindnesses toward us. As the old hymn enjoins us, 'Count your blessings'. This is sage advice regardless, for though we will never notice all of God's graces, we are greatly encouraged by noticing more and more of them. This, as we saw, leads us to repentance and thus a greater inclination to kindness. Point out the bounteous gifts of God to your children. It is a joy to make simple comments like 'Our Father made that one-of-a-kind piece of art' when looking at a sunset. Of course, you must have a mindset to be alert to these things, and that requires us to slow down in our pursuits enough to relish the blessings around us. One great irony of our lives is that we will spend money on a gourmet dinner, and then shovel down the food without savoring it. Pray for God's help to become more observant and in so doing to teach these skills to your children.

Now that we're learning to keep our eyes open for blessing, we are becoming better equipped to notice opportunities for kindness around us. We no longer miss the older woman struggling to get her groceries to her car, or the new person sitting in church whose face conveys distress. Help your children to see such opportunities as well. But go beyond just looking around you; research the ways you can minister to the poor and needy in your town and around the world. Take on a project for prayer and intervention. My family has been convicted, challenged, and moved by learning of the Rwandan genocide and the impact on children and families there. This had led us to greater concern for children in other parts of Africa, such as in northern Uganda where little ones are often cruelly conscripted to become soldiers or sex-slaves.

Awareness and education are important steps, but action is the ultimate goal. Once you are more alert to opportunities to be kind, do something! Help the woman with her groceries, or speak to the visitor at church. Pray for the poor and—you knew this was coming—give something to help. Involve your children in every aspect of these kindnesses. Children seem particularly touched by the opportunity to care for other children. Give them such opportunities. Let me stress again: this is not a matter of waiting for needs to drop in our laps, but it is our taking initiative to seek out the needs of others to commit deliberate acts of kindness.

We are indeed blessed. God's kindnesses to us are beyond number, and new every day. What joy in noticing them and giving thanks. But what greater joy we will find as we pass on the kindness to others as we are the arms and legs of Christ to a needy and sinful world.

Stepping Toward Kindness

A great way to teach kindness is to point it out to your children when you see it in your day-to-day life. Other suggestions follow below.

PRESCHOOL CHILDREN

From early on, give your little ones opportunities to help around the house. Sure, they're messy and may add time to your chores, but how much is it worth for them to learn kindness from the beginning? Engage them in helping you in your acts of kindness also.

Young children are the most closely watched, so now is the best time to catch any unkind behaviors and correct them. Habits are more easily prevented than broken.

When watching media, act upset when you see one person being mistreated by another. (Hopefully, you actually don't need to 'act' upset because it should really upset you anyway!)

Read stories showing kindnesses. The Bible contains examples. The Book of Virtues put together by William Bennett some years ago is a treasure trove of such stories.

Even young children learn kindnesses in their church classes. Making crafts to give to older church members can be a powerful experience for givers and receivers. You can think of others.

ELEMENTARY SCHOOL CHILDREN.

During family worship, take turns with each family member offering a sentence prayer thanking God for something. Continue praying until you run out of time or the ideas slow. As you pray, introduce things the children might not notice.

Encourage them to participate in a ministry project in your area, or learn about the needs in another part of the world. Have them pray regularly and even do extra chores to earn money to help with the project.

Closely watch sibling relationships, as much unkindness transpires between brothers and sisters. Keep a tight rein on teasing and other forms of disrespect.

Review the texts in this chapter as part of a focus of family worship on kindness. There are others, too, that you can find with a concordance. (Like the ESV? You may find the online resources at www.gnpcb.org/esv helpful as I have.)

Children's groups at church can organize Vacation Bible Schools for underprivileged children, or share in the church's missions conference with news on missions focusing on children, or come together for a Saturday morning to clean the church or the home of an elderly member.

TEENAGERS

Keep talking to them about speaking kindly to and about others. This, as we saw, is a particularly dangerous time.

Thank you notes and thoughtful letters are a lost art form. Have your teen join you to write notes of encouragement to church members, neighbors, or missionaries.

Point teens to their riches in Christ as their source of meaning in life, discouraging unhealthy approaches to competition in school, among friends and in sports.

As children mature, service opportunities increase. Volunteering at a hospital or nursing home, a tutoring service, or with Habitat for Humanity are just a few of the options for teens to serve their Lord.

Youth leaders can make their programs more 'fruitful' by planning activities for teens to care for others. Singing at nursing homes, repairing the homes of widows, and being big brothers and sisters to poor children are just a few.

9

GOODNESS: WHO YOU ARE
WHEN NO ONE IS AROUND

Sunday afternoons at the Patrick home were usually rather peaceful, but this particular day was much quieter than usual. Mr. Patrick was reading on the sofa, slipping in and out of consciousness as he relaxed. His wife was writing a letter to an old friend, and their three-year-old daughter was deep into her afternoon nap. Missing was the usual clamor of seven-year-old Alistair who normally took advantage of the Sabbath to chase the dog around the house or play on the floor with his toy cars, punctuating the plot with various vocal noises comprising the soundtrack of the story he was creating. His absence went unnoticed for a while before his mother noticed the silence.

'John, have you seen Alistair?' she asked her spouse.

'Not in a while,' he replied. 'Do you think he went outside to play?'

Her foray into the yard was fruitless. 'Maybe he's taking a nap,' she wondered. She went up the stairs to Alistair's room only to find the door closed. Mrs. Patrick softly turned the knob and eased the door ajar, then peeked around to spy Alistair on his knees beside his bed.

'Alistair, what are you doing?' she queried.

'Mom, I'm praying for my Sunday School teacher, Mr. Roberts.'

'Why is that, son?'

'He told us this morning that he was having surgery this week and might not be able to teach our class next week. I want God to know how much I want Mr. Roberts to be all right and to be able to teach us again soon' Alistair replied.

The tear in his mother's eye did not distract from the warm, loving smile on her face. Childlike faith has a rare beauty all its own.

What is your reaction as you read this little vignette? For most of us in the early 21st Century, it is skeptical. 'Impossible.' 'Yeah, right.' 'Come on, show me a kid like that.'

Well, I can show you a child like that, but we regrettably have to step back in time. Let me take you back to the 17th Century and the writings of James Janeway where he detailed a series of short stories of children who were remarkable in their spiritual lives. Mary A. exemplifies these little ones. Before the age of five, her commitment to Christ was clear. 'She was inclined to be much in secret prayer. And, many times, she came off from her knees with tears.'[1] Mary A. 'would choose such times and places for secret prayer as might render her less observed by others, and endeavored what she possibly could to conceal what she was doing when she was engaged in a secret duty.' She feared hypocrisy, was burdened for the souls of others, was tender and kind, gave frequent praise to God, and loved the company of faithful ministers.

This reminds us of another child who, at twelve years old, was so engrossed in discussion with spiritual men that his parents forgot him and the dialogue flowed until they returned for him. Of course, I am referring to the account of Jesus in the temple (Luke 2: 41–52). We understand this unusual behavior in Jesus, given that he was God incarnate. But how are we to comprehend Mary A.'s life? We have a difficult time imagining an adult behaving that way, much less a child.

My fear is that our disbelief unveils the shallowness of modern Christians. While we aspire to being godly, we fall short of Mary A. We look for role models to guide us toward such righteousness of life, but we search in vain. And if our faith as adults is not growing strong in these ways, how are we to show our children how to live truly good lives?

In our text in Galatians, 'goodness' comes from a word group that is similar to 'kindness' that we just examined. Since in the previous discussion we focused primarily on teaching our children to act kindly toward others, in this chapter we will concentrate on goodness as the godly character of our children. Goodness is deeper than merely good deeds, as it is rooted in the new nature given to the children of God. It is revealed most clearly when we are alone. It is the godly character and actions of our children when no one is looking.

This is a central chapter in our study, for most Christian parents work harder on the don't's of their children's behavior than on the do's. Think of children you consider to be good Christians. What likely comes to mind is that they don't use bad language, don't see bad movies, don't show disrespect to parents, or don't sneak to do naughty things. It is less natural to speak of goodness of heart and a godward focus to their lives. Yet, this inward moral character is what will carry them when they are no longer under our watch. And it is this very character that is most powerfully threatened by the powers and principalities.

We will explore how the forces of contemporary life undermine goodness in our children before reflecting further on what such goodness looks like according to Scripture. In particular, we will consider the role of suffering in cultivating biblical goodness. As is our custom, we will conclude by presenting some practical steps that should help facilitate goodness in the lives of our children.

Sin, Morals, and Values

Let's take a few moments to trace the moral changes Western culture has experienced in recent years. Most of our history has found bad deeds to be called sin, acknowledging both the existence of God and our accountability to him as his creatures. His Word was the standard for most everyone, though undoubtedly many disregarded the societal norm. Nonetheless, most folks were on the same page as we agreed on what goodness should look like, and that the standards were based in the authority of God.

As the Enlightenment convinced many people that we could work things out ourselves, the notion of sin became quaint as we were convinced human society could fend for itself with no need for a higher authority. We could devise our own standards, so sin dropped from the vocabulary and was replaced by the idea of morality. This discarded accountability to a Creator and replaced it with accountability to one's social group which scripted the morals with which one was to comply. Children learned to honor their countries and do the things that promoted a civil society, but godly character was no longer a concern.

The individualism inherent in society's development finally won the day on right and wrong. Society's morals gave way to values that the individual accepts on her own, without appeal to God or others. Now the person was accountable to no one but himself. Each person will value some things as good and bad, but no one should tell the person what those are and, conversely, you should never burden another by asking that person to live by your values. You choose your values and then live by them. No absolute values exist; only individuals can decide for themselves what to believe is right.

The problems with this have been evident in recent American political campaigns as all candidates championed what they called 'family values,' figuring most voters thought family was a good thing. Yet, the campaigns revealed a wide variety of meaning for the term 'family values.' As good as the term sounded, it carried no weight that others accepted, so it has already slipped out of the ubiquitous political rhetoric.

Modern Westerners hold only one 'value' to be applied to every person, and that is tolerance. Tolerance is extolled explicitly and implicitly at every turn in the media and popular culture—and even in more pulpits than we'd like to think. Since there is no objective right or wrong, we ought not to tell others what they ought and ought not to do (strange sentence, but it shows the self-contradictory thinking in this). Nothing outside the individual obligates a person to act in a certain way, so we simply have nothing to say to the other that carries any authority. This trend is so strong that 67% of Americans do not believe in any moral absolutes,[2] a number that obviously includes many professing Christians.

There is a place for tolerance. We do well to honor differing cultures in their art forms, languages, and such. My Pakistani neighbors till a style of garden that is not typical for our neighborhood, and I can tolerate that. But values of right and wrong are a different story. As has often been said, the Ten Commandments are not God's ten 'suggestions'. Christianity has long held the truth of God's Laws to be absolute and authoritative, though this position is under heavy attack from within and without the ranks of the faithful.

The move to tolerance as the only virtue coincides with the shift of focus from a person's 'character' to his 'personality'. Historically, a person of character was one with strong convictions, usually Christian, whose life demonstrated them in every aspect. Parents worked diligently in an effort to raise children of character. Now, personality rules. We focus on trying to demonstrate personal qualities that will make others like us and thus promote our self-interests. As David Wells astutely observes, 'Character is good or bad, while personality is attractive, forceful, or magnetic. Attention [shifted] from the moral virtues, which need to be cultivated, to the image, which needs to be fashioned.'[3] When confronted with adversity or suffering, a person of character perseveres and deepens. The person focused on personality sees hard times as a call for a 'makeover' to upgrade an image, giving little thought to the rights or wrongs of the situation.

The shallowness of our culture's language about sin and character conspire to thwart, and sometimes seduce, Christian parents who want godly children. The Christian message is tamed to be a mere opinion, or a lifestyle, which is okay for you if you want it, but it is certainly not one that authoritatively stakes a claim on anyone else's life. Even if you are not teaching this to your children, they are hearing it every day from various sources and thus may believe this nonetheless.

So, the first way the culture undermines the notion of goodness in our children is to undermine the notion of goodness itself. Why go to the trouble of cultivating character when there is no authoritative reason to do so, and when everyone around you doesn't bother to do so, and even discourages you from the task?

One visible result of these trends is the apathy we show toward wrong. Even if we see a behavior in another as sinful, we are unaffected. Notice how easily we can hear God's Name taken in vain in a movie without being offended. Contrast that with the Israelites of the Old Testament who would not even speak the Name of God out of reverence, much less sit idly by as others profaned it. We have lost what William Kirkpatrick calls moral indignation. He explains, 'When tolerance is the sole virtue, students' capacity for moral indignation, so important for moral development, is severely inhibited.[4] Yet the idea of tolerance not only discourages moral indignation, it undermines it and makes it an evil in itself.

How then are we to raise 'good' children if there is no concept of good? And how can we promote good without teaching that there is also sin which should offend us even as it offends our holy God? The first threat to goodness in our children is the campaign against the very idea of goodness.

Then there are the ever present pressures of childhood. When we reviewed the collapse of character into personality, we saw that moral integrity is out and image is in, image which portrays one's unique personality—or at least the personality one seeks to portray given the shallow meaning of the term. It is no surprise then that the pressure to 'look' a certain way is now the number one pressure reported by young people (with 69% citing it as a challenge). Image is everything—a stark contrast to God who doesn't look on the outward but on the inward. Yet the right clothes, music, stride, and attitude are important if a young person wants to be tolerated in a youth culture that is hypocritically intolerant of those who look or act different from the prescribed standards. This is followed by the more traditional pressures of sex, alcohol, and drugs. While teens adamantly defend their peers by saying they do not pressure them, the truth is otherwise. And the pressure imposed is not to be good, but to be 'cool' in image and behavior. There seems to be more agreement on what 'cool' is than on what goodness is among young people, and there is great social pressure to conform to it. All of this is worsened as it is reinforced by the media who aggressively hawk the products that are supposed to help you achieve your social goals. Where social pressure has worked to promote goodness in the past, it now disregards it and replaces it with meaningless social and fashion norms required to fit in with the group. These pressures not only apply to teens, but press downward to younger and younger children as even very young children feel the need to wear certain brands, have a cell phone, and to be 'thin' to fit the image of the popular person.

This means that it is compelling for children to devote their energies to pursuit of social acceptability and personal image rather than to spiritual growth in their relationships with God and the development of goodness. We as caring adults do well to look in the mirror on these issues as we experience social pressures to live in certain neighborhoods, drive particular types of autos, and to have the latest electronic gadgets. We must model a difference if our children are to be different.

The last threat to goodness I want to reflect on is the frequent focus of parents on children's bad behaviors without teaching the notion of character. Many Christian parenting books seem to relish teaching better and better ways to punish your children when they are bad (or increasingly, to affirm their self-esteem when they are bad). There is no doubt Scripture encourages us to punish wayward children. Yet, as I observed in a previous work, discipline relates to disciples, and it is a developing of character within a relationship not merely a pointing out of shortcomings. No amount of saying 'no' to children will promote goodness. Children merely learn to be more clandestine so as to avoid discovery and thus punished unless they also learn the virtues of the Christian life. Combining the two will prepare a place for the Spirit to plant the fruit of goodness. It is important to understand more of this idea of goodness as we seek to promote it in our lives and the lives of our children, so let us consider what Scripture has to say.

Goodness in the Bible

All the fruits listed in Galatians 5 are rooted in the character of God. Here is why the issue of character ultimately matters: God is holy and calls us to share his holiness of character (Lev. 11: 44–5). Holiness involves being set apart in character and thus being like God in righteousness not just on occasion, but always. Specific acts of goodness do not suffice; character—who one is when no one is around—matters as that is what God is like in all circumstances.

Goodness is an attribute of God's character (Exod. 33: 19; 1 Kgs 8: 66; 2 Chron. 6: 41; Ps. 31: 19; 65: 4; Isa. 63: 7; Jer. 31: 12; Hos. 3: 5) most famously noted in Psalm 23: 6 as David knew the goodness of God would follow him throughout his life. Knowing God is and will always be good to us is wonderful incentive to be good ourselves.

Followers of God reflect his goodness. In Romans 15: 14, Paul notes the Roman Christians to be full of goodness. Such goodness ideally comes not by compulsion of being made to be good, but out of free will (Philem. 1: 14). Consider the difference between a four-year-old who pouts as she shares her cookies with her brother after her mother insists she do so, to this same act done with joy and spontaneity out of love for the brother. Goodness is not forced from without, but flows from the heart that God has changed. This is, after all, what makes it a fruit of the Spirit.

Scripture says little directly about what produces goodness, though it is safe to say it results from faithful obedience and abiding in Christ and his love for us. It is the moral aspect of having the mind of Christ (1 Cor. 2: 16). It is thus not taught directly, but learned in our day-to-day walk with Christ and through being with others who are good. For parents, this means promoting goodness in our children is a long-term project, not a 'three easy steps' thing (though wouldn't that be nice!).

Now being good is challenge enough, but we must realize that goodness will bring suffering (Matt. 5: 10–11). The role of suffering in the Christian life is a tragically overlooked topic in modern Christian literature. Christ, of course, is the only truly and completely good person to grace the earth, and as a result he suffered, both during his life and in giving it. It seems strange to those of us accustomed to modern evangelistic techniques that God's words to Ananias, as he prepared him to talk with Saul the new convert, told him of how much Saul would suffer for the name of Christ (Acts 9: 16). Without a doubt, the rest of the New Testament story bears out how much Paul suffered for his Lord and Savior, and how he taught that suffering is normative in the life of the believer (Phil. 1: 29).

This same Paul later admonishes us to pursue (Phil. 3: 10) and rejoice in suffering inasmuch as it is the door through which we pass to know more of God's grace (Rom. 5: 3–5), including the development of character and hope. Being good will lead to suffering, but suffering will build Christlike character, which will of course produce more suffering, and so the life of growth in Christ continues. Yet, we live in a day when we are allergic to suffering, and when many Christian authorities, taking a cue from advertising techniques, sell the gospel as the way to escape suffering in this life rather than as a promise of suffering in this life for the sake of Christ's Name and glory now and for eternity. For our present sufferings lead us to be glorified in Christ and are not even worth comparing to the greatness of such glory (Rom. 8: 17–18).

If we reflect for a moment, this makes sense. Say a child is learning to play the piano. He will miss some activities with friends, some television programs, and lots of Internet time for the sake of practice. This is, in a sense, suffering. He will have to contend with chiding from friends who don't choose the path of discipline. This young man will face many hours of frustration as new fingerings and passages don't come easily to him. He must persevere in this path by rejecting all the allure of immediate gratifications that call to him every day. He could forego his ambition to be an excellent pianist and avoid all this suffering. Yet, should he endure, the day will come when the great joy of playing beautiful music and blessing others who listen will more than compensate for the hardships involved.

We understand this process in many areas. Other disciplines such as athletics, intellectual endeavors, and dance require similar processes. Yet somehow we do not see how growth in the Christian life will involve the same pattern. I recall from my graduate school days that a loose translation for the New Testament term 'diligent' was to 'bust a gut', showing the effort and energy involved in living for Christ, a great and more comprehensive diligence than is required for other areas of mastery, and one that will involve facing greater opposition and hostility. We are now a long way from the idea of tolerance, for tolerance will not lead down this biblical path to goodness and glory. Very few Mary A.'s are around today because most believers shy away from the biblical path to goodness.

Moving toward Goodness

Please allow me to share a few general ideas of what parents and others who care for children can do to promote goodness in the next generation.

The reader can probably already pick up the hints to my first suggestion, which is to reject tolerance as 'the' value. Yes, we must be tolerant of others in areas outside the realm of what is right and wrong, but we cannot be spiritually neutralized by this value that saps our moral indignation and aborts its development in our children. Learn to critique the propaganda of pluralism and to present proper behavior as rooted in God's Nature, not in personal opinion.

Similarly, let's watch our language a bit more closely. Words evolve naturally, but we do well to bear in mind the impact of this when it works against the cause of Christ. Don't be shy to use the word 'sin' and to eschew the term 'values'. Be explicit with your children that you pray for their character with less emphasis on personality.

Continuing a pulse that runs throughout this book, we must deliberately counter the media propaganda. Children of Christian parents must learn that they are different while we show them the superficiality of popular trends and expectations. I am less concerned about exactly where the line is for how much children should conform to culture than I am about the notion that they want to be different. I'm reminded of the short-sighted teen prayer that God stop his physical relationship with his girlfriend when it becomes wrong, while he really hopes God lets him go as far as possible before miraculously stopping it. Of course, the proper approach is to be seeking God as to please him and in that context attitudes about physical expression of affection are altered dramatically. Even so, we should be committed to following Christ and focused on that rather than on how much culture we can consume without drawing God's wrath.

Children watch our lives more than we think, so our goodness (or lack of it) is always on display for them. Here is a curious danger. Our children see celebrities on television in carefully crafted images with lots of makeup, but don't see the celebrities when they're at home with their guards down. This makes it easier to see them as heroes. In contrast, they see parents when they first get up, when they've had a bad day, and when they simply don't feel well. While this means they'll know more of our failures, it also means they can see true goodness in the real world without makeup.

If we say there are absolutes in the world, then it is best if our children see that others hold tightly to them as well. The community of faith is vital here. We need churches that are not shy to preach about sin, about right and wrong, about goodness, and even about suffering. How much more powerful is God's truth in our children's lives when the community of God's people demonstrates it in real life. Church leaders are challenged humbly to assess their strategies before God to see whether marketing techniques are replacing God's truth as their strategy for building the church.

Above all, we must pray for our children. Pray for their protection from the pressures of the world and the anesthetizing morality of tolerance. We must fervently seek God's grace to build character in their lives by the work of the Holy Spirit and his fruit of goodness.

Guidelines to Goodness

I've tried to show that goodness does not come as the result of simple techniques, but is cultivated in the daily challenges of life. Nonetheless, the following suggestions may help you make some changes that will help.

PRESCHOOLERS

Don't be shy to point out when they do wrong, but be just as quick to praise them when they do right. Goodness leads ultimately to glory, so let them taste it early.

Discourage them from wanting and getting toys and clothes that they see advertised on television by exposing the lie that these will make them happy. Skepticism in this arena can't start too young.

Teach them to pray when you are not there. Explain how they can talk to God while on their beds going to sleep, and how to rest in him when alone. Teach from early on that God is there when no one else is looking. If they are taught this is a time to turn to him, it might pre-empt negative uses of these opportunities.

Pray alone, with your spouse, and with other parents for wisdom in how to promote goodness in a tolerant culture.

ELEMENTARY-AGED CHILDREN

Take advantage of daily events to teach goodness. When they tell of a friend's naughty actions, ask them what that friend would have done differently if she was seeking to please God when others were not looking. When they are good (or not), talk through how this did or did not promote God's glory.

Let them know early the costs of being a Christian. Tell the stories of those who suffered for faith. Biblical stories like Daniel and his three friends are great examples of being good when it goes against the culture, and how God delivers his children.

Continue promoting good literature for your children. Christian biographies are wonderful sources of role models, for example.

Promote friendships with people of different ages who demonstrate goodness. Time with elder saints is powerful, but so is companionship with teenagers who are truly Christ's servants.

Afford children opportunities to serve others in the church by pointing out simple needs (opening doors, picking up dropped Bibles) and involving them formally with ministry to widows, the poor, and other needy people.

TEENAGERS

B ear in mind that teens will learn to decide for themselves as they have more freedom. Give them some room for this by not being oppressively strict. Yet, build communication so the teen can discuss his successes and failures with you. Give them chances to prove your trust in them is deserved, yet be patient with failures.

Continue intergenerational relationships. Teens learn much from watching college students, but also learn to admire elder Christians when they spend time with them.

Parents should take the lead in family worship times and other occasions to teach them the biblical philosophy of life, and how following Christ produces suffering which works to God's glory. Limit-setting won't be enough at this age; they need to understand more of God's plan. The first verses of Romans 5 are a great starting place.

Teens are particularly sensitive to hypocrisy, so don't neglect your own spiritual life as they watch you during these difficult years.

Involve them in activities with other adults in the church, such as pastors, elders, deacons, and women's ministry leaders so they see goodness at work in these lives and have a greater appreciation of goodness in the community of faith.

10

TRUE TILL THE END: FAITHFULNESS

Frodo[1] stood on the banks of the Anduin, reflecting on how far he had come and pondering what was to come. How did all of this happen to him? He wished none of it had. What was going to become of him? What was going to become of Middle Earth? Did he have even the slightest chance of succeeding? These questions assaulted his mind, but he could not heed them. He had been given a task and was going to complete it as best he could, even if it took his life. And the only way he could do this was alone. Or so he thought.

He gathered his resolve and set off to cross the river in one of the elven boats. He didn't want to meet with any of his comrades, or be seen by them as he left, so he put on the Ring. The Fellowship had suffered so much on his account that he desired to—no—had to complete the journey to destroy the Ring by himself.

Then he heard a voice calling to him. It was Sam, who was determined to follow Frodo to the ends of the earth. Frodo knew Sam wouldn't understand the burden he bore. Sam, in his desperation, called for Frodo to wait, but Frodo would not take notice. He pressed on. Sam continued, 'Not alone! Frodo!'

'Stay back, Sam!' Frodo called, looking over his shoulder at his friend. 'I'm going to Mordor alone.'

'Of course you are, and I'm coming with you!' Sam replied. Realizing Frodo would not wait, he leapt into the water. Frodo called after him, 'You can't swim!' he saw Sam's curly head go under. 'Sam!' he wheeled the boat round and pulled Sam up out of the water by his hair. 'I'm drownded, Mr. Frodo! Save me!'

'Up you go, Sam, my lad! Here, take my hand!'

'I can't see your hand!'

'Here, here it is!' Frodo said, taking the Ring off now.

Once Sam was safely into the boat, he explained his reason for following Frodo in brief, but powerful words, 'I made a promise, Mr. Frodo, a promise! I said I wasn't going to leave you, and I don't mean to. I don't mean to.'

'Oh, Sam. Come on, then.'

Frodo could not resist such determination. This pair would have many adventures together, and Frodo would further learn of Sam's simple wisdom. If Sam had not been faithful, Frodo's mission would have failed. He would have been deceived and made helpless by the creature Gollum, if not killed. The Ring would have gone into the hands of the Enemy and the whole of Middle Earth would be lost. A faithful friend made all the difference.

Many of us vividly recall this moving scene from Tolkien's timeless *Lord of the Rings* trilogy, whether by reading it or seeing the cinematic adaptation. It touches in us a longing to be true like Sam, and to have others as true to us. We'll see in the next chapter that there are many today who do not value gentleness, but few will argue that faithfulness is not a virtue. Be it faithfulness to one's sports team, an Islamic jihad, the pursuit of success, or even to 'being who you are', people today aspire to faithfulness to something, if not some one. As Christians, we know faithfulness is at its root a fruit of the Spirit, a reflection of the One who is ever and unfailingly faithful.

Yet, fictional stories of faithfulness move us because it is rare to see it in the 'real world' today. This is regrettably true even in Christian circles. We long to be faithful and to raise children who are faithful to God and to others, but we see little around us to emulate. Let us look more closely at our times to see why faithfulness is rare before we examine the nature of biblical faithfulness more closely.

'To Thine Own Self Be True': Cultural Threats to Faithfulness

These famous words from Hamlet summarize the philosophy of our times. Postmodernism breeds cynicism about anything outside or even inside ourselves. What is truth anyway? So, you might as well be true to yourself if anything. (Some postmodern thinkers see no reason for valuing one's self either!) If being yourself means forsaking your marriage, then it is not only permissible, it is your duty. If stepping on a co-worker is the only way to get that promotion, then step away. Your colleague would do the same to you, right? If being a popular teen requires the use of crude language or cursing, then God will understand. These exemplify the many doors such thinking opens, and all of them lead away from God.

The cause of faithfulness was in danger in the Western world even before postmodernism filtered down into popular culture. In the United States in particular, the blurring of biblical truth with civic values led to placing great value on individual freedom. The sixties saw the popular exploitation of this as freedom meant sex should be loosed from the bonds of marital relationships, and the pursuit of pleasure should not be inhibited by laws restricting the use of certain substances.

The cause of freedom also discourages making or keeping commitments such as the need to marry someone who impregnated you or is carrying your baby. Just a week before I wrote this, new statistics were published that say 40% of babies born in the United States have unmarried mothers, and this is despite the decrease in number of teenagers having babies out of wedlock. The great increase is women in their twenties who choose this rather than be tied down to a marriage. We learn how to think this way from the widespread stories of celebrities having babies born of relationships of convenience. The media rejoices in these births, validating the idea that having children serves to fulfill a desire to nurture or fulfill a selfish need, giving little thought to the need for two active parents and a great deal of commitment to get through colic-filled nights of wailing by cute babies who will grow to place differing demands on their parent(s).

Marital vows are opposed to such freedom as well, and the right and even mandate to be true to oneself overrules these in many cases, spouses departing from relationships which hinder their careers and aspirations. Or, as is particularly the case with celebrity role models, couples will simply choose to live together so long as they both find that makes them happy. Children are the losers, as we've seen, with a million children in the US alone watching their parents' marriages blow up annually since the 1970's. These statistics should improve, however, as fewer children are born into marriages in the first place. Fathers are particularly culpable, as some 25% of children now have no real relationship with a father[2]. As sexual intercourse has so effectively been divorced from its biological purpose of procreation, so has donating sperm been detached from fathering a child in the sense of faithful commitment to relationship. Many children never know their fathers, and are soon joined by children whose fathers sail into the sunset of their lives after a divorce, often encouraged to do so by bitter mothers.

Faithfulness is undermined in other areas by the relentless message of advertisements. First, simply the diversification of choices discourages what used to be called 'brand loyalty'. Even if you stick with a brand, it evolves into different colors, strengths, and additives. Things as mundane as dishwashing detergents and toothpastes now compete for our money with new varieties, discouraging loyalty to an old faithful.

Commercialism thrives on impulse buying, and so many themes of advertisements strike against being true to something you have. 'Act now', 'Call within the next 15 minutes', and 'Just do it' illustrate the trend to forsake the old and grab the new without much thought. Industry accommodates this mindset by making products increasingly disposable. Television on the blink? Buy a new, improved one rather than fix the old one. Technology pushes such thinking. Even as I type this on my 'old' computer, I know that a faster, more reliable one could replace it for far less than it would take to make improvements on the one I have. But relationships aren't products, and technology doesn't improve them. The disposability of our products affects our approach to relationships. As soon as one is a little inconvenient, toss it and try a new one.

The advertising industry also strikes at faithfulness by its generous definition of truth. Parents and children both live in a culture that has grown cynical with the outrageous claims of commercials and the products they flaunt. We know that buying a certain car won't make us super-sexy, nor will watching a particular television program change our lives. Moreover, the power of the image in media supplants the notion of truth. One must defend a statement that something is true while images carry no truth claim but compel us nonetheless. The clever and compelling images of advertisements deceive us even as they are unfaithful to the truth of what the product can do for us.

The assault on the value of the spoken or written word is also carried on through politicians who offer empty promises and then skirt the truth when confronted with their misdeeds. Even the church has been rocked by scandals as Christian leaders are exposed as hypocrites. Excuses abound for not fulfilling our commitments and promises. No wonder our children struggle to tell the truth in our day, and no wonder we long for 'Sams' in our lives.

Freedom also impacts the workplace. There is little company loyalty these days. A slightly higher salary or better benefits is about all it takes to lure a person from one company to another. Make the offer a little better, and it justifies leaving your home town with your relatives, church, and the friendships your children have made. Pastors seem more 'led' to churches with higher pay than to smaller, struggling churches. Such mobility increases income, but leaves nuclear families without roots and relationships, increasing the stress on that family and increasing the chances of it, too, coming unglued. It also communicates that money and success are more important than faithfulness.

In contrast, most children seem drawn to familiar places and faces. They value security and assume the family to be totally safe. Uprooting families, though sometimes indeed necessary, shakes children's sense of faithfulness, though not as severely as does divorce. One of the most profound things I have seen in my counseling practice is how hard it is for children to even imagine that their family could experience a divorce. When they go through it, the security and faithfulness of their entire world is brought into question.

The 'rat race' of our times makes it easy for Christians to become caught in this constant change so being faithful isn't given much thought or, if it is considered, it takes second place to the 'benefits' changes are thought to bring. We easily take on these worldly values and give a back seat to faithfulness.

All of this can leave children feeling betrayed by parents for their unfaithfulness. As they grow, these boys and girls will turn to friends for faithfulness. It is tragic how often they turn to the wrong kinds of friends. Cruelty to friends via betrayal and back-stabbing are commonplace these days as children adapt the values of their parents and are willing to hurt others to improve their status. Some children then turn to the underachieving group who are most accepting provided you put no pressure on them (or they on you) to better yourselves in any way. Many 'good' kids thus turn to these groups for friendships to the chagrin of their parents, finding some measure of dependability, even at the cost of their own performance in school and pursuit of the things of God. It is not a good friend who does not encourage you to grow (as seen in Sam going with Frodo rather than chiding him for inconveniencing himself), but short of finding true and faithful friends, these shallow yet intense relationships often meet the 'felt needs' of many of our children—needs felt because of a lack of more faithful alternatives.

What then does true faithfulness look like? And how can we guide our children into being faithful Christians in all the roles of their lives? Let us now focus on these urgent questions.

Faithfulness Brought to Life

Though it has been our common practice to review biblical teachings on most of the fruit of the Spirit we have reviewed thus far, this time we take a different tact. We will reflect on a few biblical stories of individuals who model faithfulness in their lives. In doing so, we will focus on several vital dimensions where we long to be faithful, and to promote faithfulness in the children under our care.

Being Faithful to the One Who Is Truly Faithful

The faithfulness of God is taught and praised throughout the Bible. It is his faithfulness that compels us to be faithful as we seek to be like him. Possibly Deuteronomy best captures the heart of this when in chapter 7 God has Moses speak to the people. He admonishes them that, when God brings them into the Promised Land, they are to remember that 'it was not because you were more in number that the Lord set his love on you and chose you…, but it is because the Lord loves you and is keeping the oath that he swore to your fathers' (vv. 7–8). 'Know therefore that the Lord your God is God, the faithful God who keeps covenant and steadfast love with those who love him and keep his commandments, to a thousand generations' (v. 9).

God initially takes Abram, makes a covenant with him, and proceeds to work this out through the children of Israel and all people of true faith in God. Biblical history is the story of God's faithfulness to his people, of his keeping his promise despite repeated and severe breeches of the agreement by his sinful people. Such faithfulness by God justifies his call to his people also to be faithful to the covenant (Deut. 28: 1) and to one another. Throughout the prophetic books, God, even as he announces his harrowing judgments on unfaithful Israel, remains faithful to his promise, a promise realized in the coming of Jesus and in his death and resurrection. In this, we learn the essence of faithfulness is commitment to a promise regardless of the response of others. It is not a matter of convenience or feeling appreciated; rather, it is an expression of the character of the one who is faithful.

Many examples might be cited of individuals in the Bible who were also faithful to God. Indeed, Hebrews 11 is a tribute to many of these believers. But maybe Paul's testimony will best serve to show the nature of true Spirit-given faithfulness. Paul recites his 'spiritual resume' as he is challenged as an apostle, not just to be boasting. Paul recounts his story in 2 Corinthians 11: 23–8:

> …countless beatings, and often near death. Five times
> I received at the hands of the Jews the forty lashes less one.
> Three times I was beaten with rods. Once I was stoned.

> Three times I was shipwrecked; a night and a day I was
> adrift at sea; on frequent journeys, in danger from rivers,
> danger from robbers, danger from my own people, danger
> from Gentiles, danger in the city, danger in the wilderness,
> danger at sea, danger from false brothers; in toil and
> hardship, through many a sleepless night, in hunger and
> thirst, often without food, in cold and exposure. And, apart
> from other things, there is the daily pressure on me of my
> anxiety for all the churches.

I can hardly type these words without memories of Frodo
and Sam's experiences flashing through my head. Yet Paul's
suffering was not fiction or fantasy; it was genuine. How easy
might it have been to have turned back under such adversity!
Even with all this behind him, in the next verses he confesses
his weaknesses, of which he will boast in if he is to boast.

Then consider how many of us as Christians behave today.
We complain if the temperature at church is not just right; we
consider being late for dinner after Sunday worship as hardship.
We feel justified in not praying so we can watch a beloved
television program or grab some extra sleep. We are faithful in
that we believe we are saved from hell and headed for eternity
with God. But we are decidedly not faithful in the ways Paul
was, nor even in the gritty perseverance of Sam and Frodo.

This reminds me of a visit years ago to some Mayan ruins
in Mexico. We toured a place called the ball court, a large
field with a wall on either side, these being some twenty-five
feet high. Near the top of each wall, in the middle of the field,
was a circle of stone that stood perpendicular to the wall, with
an open area in the midst of it. It faintly resembled a sideways
basketball hoop made of stone. Teams would play for several
days on end to try to get the ball through the appropriate hoop,
first score winning the game. This was somewhat mundane
until the guide explained the 'prize' for the scorer of the winning
goal: to be sacrificed to the gods. Whoa, now! Maybe sacrifice
a loser, but this racked my comfortable Western sensibility.

Then I thought for a minute. What would it say to the gods to
give them a loser? And what would it say of the worshippers that
they would work hard to avoid being sacrificed to the god whom
they served? No, sacrifice was an honor. More recently this
reminds me of how some radical Islamist groups are training

their children: martyrdom is the most glorious aspiration, dying in service to Mohammed. Yes, this is perverted religion when the goal is to kill innocent people as you commit suicide. Nonetheless, there is a faithfulness found in this that is strangely missing in much Western Christianity. I am, however, honored to say that our brothers and sisters in other parts of the world choose persecution and suffering daily for the sake of the true faith. Christian faithfulness is not lost, it has just disappeared in the haze of Western prosperity and comfort.

Such faithfulness in our day can be seen in many lives of folks who will never be on the front page. One example is a missionary family we have known for many years. Mack and Doris Graham have served, with their children, for several decades with Wycliffe Bible Translators in Papua New Guinea. They have endured the near death of a child with malaria, the burning of their house, betrayal by tribespeople who were supposed to be helping with translation, and immensely slow and tedious work. Somehow they have stayed and endured, becoming living testimony to God's strength in their lives which gives them such unnatural faithfulness to their calling.

Even though we say we know such service is what Christ calls us to, we still evangelize children with the simple promise of heaven and little attention to the cost to be counted. We have seen that suffering is part of the faith, but hiding from that makes faith impotent in the face of hardship, and faithfulness is redefined as something easy, like regular church attendance, and not the radical commitment and sacrifice of Paul and other heroes and heroines of the faith.

FAITHFUL TO THE FAMILY

The life of ease promised by technology and advertising is a lie, and nowhere is this more evident in what is required to have healthy relationships with others who, like us, still struggle with sin. We reviewed the toll this takes on marriages and on the faithfulness of parents—particularly fathers—to their children after divorce. Let us be refreshed by biblical examples of faithfulness to family.

Several wonderful stories come to mind. Consider Ruth, a mere daughter-in-law to Naomi, and widowed at that. No blood ties existed to compel her to stay with Naomi as she set out for her homeland. Ruth's words of commitment make Sam's seem shallow:

> For where you go I will go, and where you lodge I will lodge. Your people shall be my people, and your God my God. Where you die I will die, and there will I be buried. May the Lord do so to me and more also if anything but death parts me from you.
>
> Ruth 1: 16–17

The rest of the book shows she meant it, and that God honored her for it.

Marital faithfulness was used as a metaphor for God's in the moving story of Hosea who took and was faithful to an incorrigibly unfaithful wife, Gomer (Hos. 1). No easy, no fault divorce for Hosea. We also easily overlook the great faithfulness of Joseph to his 'fiancé' Mary who would have been held guiltless by those around him if he called off the marriage when he learned his betrothed was pregnant (Matt. 1: 18–25).

I was recently teaching a course on abnormal psychology at a state university, and showed a video clip of a couple who talked about coping with the husband's schizophrenia. The woman admitted their marriage was not as planned, but that they had grown through it nonetheless. A student responded afterward that she could not handle being married to someone who had such problems. I commented that she should take care not to take vows such as 'for better or worse' or 'in sickness and in health' if she felt that way. To my shock, the class burst out into applause. Even in this setting, most still see faithfulness as a virtue.

This young woman's attitude dramatically contrasts with a recent example of faithfulness to a spouse, that of J. Robertson McQuilken, former President of Columbia International University in South Carolina. I had the honor of sitting under this fine man years ago as a student there in 1978. But a few years after I had moved on, his wife was diagnosed with Alzheimer's Disease. Though he had a vital ministry as a Christian college president, her need for care was great as her health and alertness slowly deteriorated. He made the astonishing decision to resign his post to be with her, despite urging to the contrary by many of his colleagues. Most of us know how demanding such care can be, cleaning up after incontinence, coping with outbursts of anger, and all for someone who no longer even recognizes you. It was twenty years before Muriel McQuilken succumbed to this dreaded disease. After two decades of such earthy care for his wife, Dr. McQuilken said in an interview after her death that he did not feel he had given anything up, but had merely served God as he had been asked to serve.[3] Examples of faithfulness are still among us, and let us pray that we can point our children to such models and even be them ourselves, praying that our children will be blessed by God's Spirit with this striking, countercultural fruit in our families.

FAITHFUL AS A FRIEND

Children, especially as they grow into teenagers, naturally long for good friends. We've already seen how our culture makes it challenging to find a good friend, even as we are touched by the example of faithful friendship in Tolkien's story.

Possibly the greatest tale of true and faithful friendship comes from God's Word, and of course that is the wonderful account of Jonathan and David. 1 Samuel 18 is the pivot of the story. The heart of this friendship is described in the beautiful language of Scripture, 'the soul of Jonathan was knit to the soul of David, and Jonathan loved him as his own soul' (v. 1). This compelled the friends to make a covenant in the verses that followed. As we know, Jonathan risked his life to protect David from the vengeful jealousy of his own father. No shallow, comfortable relationship is seen here. No sharing in common passivity and just 'hanging out'. This friendship was costly and dangerous, as friendship should be, and as our children should be taught that it is.

It is one of the great joys in my life that I have a true friend, though it is an improbable friendship. Michael and I have known each other for over thirty years. We have prayed together, had Bible studies, gone on trips, enjoyed concerts and sporting events, and met for meals regularly. It is an improbable friendship first because Michael is an African-American, and such friendships were not vogue in the 1970s in the southern part of the United States when we first befriended one another. Both his family and mine had some discomfort with it. Our friendship was even less likely when I moved to California for my graduate training, and then to a city still hundreds of miles from Michael. But Michael is faithful. He visited me in California at some expense, and helped drive the truck when I moved back east. He has prayed for me and my family through these many years, and his heartfelt prayers still bring my father to tears. When there has been an illness in my family, Michael was there. Undaunted by distance or racial differences, Michael is first of all a child of God, but one who lives God's faithfulness in his role as a friend. It is a special blessing to have such a friend.

As our children make friends, it is incumbent upon us as parents to provide good groups of peers for them to choose from through our churches and Christian friends. Ideally, we live good friendships before their eyes that stand in contrast to the 'soap opera' relationships they will encounter in school and other places. We do well to teach them the true nature and value of faithful friendship to others as they face difficult times with their friends, and wisely to choose friends that will encourage their faith.

FAITHFUL TO OUR WORD

Sam stressed to Frodo that he was intent on keeping a promise he had made, and such is a faint reflection of the promises God has made to his people which he so faithfully keeps. Today's world holds little esteem for keeping promises or honoring one's word. Yet, our Christian hope is completely built on belief in God's faithfulness to his Word.

Scripture stresses keeping one's word, from Hannah's giving Samuel to the Lord in 1 Samuel 1 to the heart wrenching faithfulness of Jephthah (Judges 11) who vowed to give to God a burnt offering of the first thing out of his door upon his return from victory over the Ammonites. As you recall, this turned out to be his only child, his beloved daughter. How easily we could come up with excuses for him to find a way around this, yet Jephthah does not flinch in his intent to fulfill his vow, and he follows through on his word. The lesson of Scripture is more toward being careful in what you say than in making excuses when promises come back to haunt you. Imagine if we took our word this seriously in our day. We would be much slower to speak than we often are.

As parents, we must demonstrate this type of clear communication, letting our 'yes' be yes and our 'no' be no, as James 5: 12 admonishes us. We tend to do rather well in taking children places we promise, but are more likely to fail in not following through with promised punishments. If you say your child will be grounded if she comes home late, and then don't follow through, you are being unfaithful to God and to your child. What you might perceive as mercy is actually undermining your child's trust in you. So, don't promise if you don't plan to follow through. Similarly, we must teach our children to do the same, both toward us and toward others.

I hope this reflection has deepened your convictions about faithfulness to God, family, friends, and your word in your own life as one who follows Christ and cares for children. Please take some time to think about examples of faithful people in your life and to thank God for them. Pray that God will show you how to take the ideas in this chapter and change you to be a bearer of more abundant fruit of faithfulness. Then, consider some of the following suggestions to help your children stand against the threats to faithfulness and to be cultivated to bear faithful fruit themselves.

Fashioning Faithful Children

There are no 'three easy steps' to faithfulness. It may be 'caught' from parents as much as 'taught' by actions. Still, the following may prove helpful.

PRESCHOOLERS

Be aware that fallen children will often go through a phase in the preschool years of trying out their new developmental skill of saying things that are not true. It is important that they quickly learn that lying is a sin and is therefore punished.

That is best accomplished when they learn early that we are people of our word. Don't tease with the truth or exploit the naivety of young children. Be honest and straightforward in communication.

Faithful relationships can be learned from brothers and sisters. See that they treat one another with respect and learn to empathize with one another. This requires close monitoring and actively correcting disrespectful remarks and teaching faithful ways of interacting, including keeping promises and spending time with each other.

By now it is clear how important stories are to young children. Share stories of faithful friendships and faithful followers of God. Biblical stories like that of Jonathan and David are the place to start, but seek out other stories that reinforce the point. *The Book of Virtues* and its kin are again helpful.

Teach children faithfulness to the church by regular attendance and commitment to caring for one another as members. The community of believers is a marvelous setting to learn all the dimensions of faithfulness we have discussed.

ELEMENTARY AGE CHILDREN

This is an important age for children to develop faithful friendships. Choose the contexts where they will find friends carefully. You place them in certain schools, or classes, or clubs, or teams, and do so with the goal of putting them around children who would make good friends, even as you coach your children on being good friends to others.

Even at this age it is important through family devotions and worship to teach children what marriage is like and the importance of faithfulness in family relationships. This might well be demonstrated by the way you and your spouse care for your ageing parents.

Be faithful to your children by spending good time with them playing games, reading, and going places together. Watching television or movies does not count.

Point out God's faithfulness to you, your child, and your family in day-to-day events such as providing food, shelter, and clothing, in protecting from harm and illness, in giving you minds that read the Scriptures and understand something of the nature of God. Contrast this with the things they hear on commercials about what they need, and teach them to be cynical about the truth-value of advertising.

Teach children routines for chores and devotions as a way of laying the groundwork for being faithful in daily activities and not ruled by feelings and impulse.

TEENAGERS

Take the initiative to ask questions about what they think makes for a good friend, and how to be one themselves. Clarify any misconceptions based on Scriptural faithfulness, and help your children think through their real-life friendships in light of this. Learning to evaluate friendships is a vital tool they will carry throughout life.

Spend time teaching younger teens especially about marriage and what is takes. Actively point out and critique cultural ideas about relationships. Cast a vision for the joy of faithful marriages including parenting children, support in hardships, and even the possibilities of caring for a spouse through illness or the later years of life.

Keep firm on limits you set. Curfews should be clear and not just estimates, and strictly enforced. Teach them your trust in them will grow with their faithfulness in keeping curfews and being responsible. Future privileges are earned by faithfulness, not pressuring you.

Encourage your teenager to take on a responsibility at church or in the community. This could be singing in the choir, helping with a children's program, tutoring an underprivileged child, or visiting a nursing home. Make this a priority that isn't missed for frivolous reasons.

Model faithfulness to them by spending time with them, staying invested in their relationships by knowing their friends, and supporting them through the normal challenges of growing up. Be an encourager to them, not just a critic.

For teens and younger children as well, be faithful in prayer for their spiritual protection and growth.

11

IT'S TOUGH TO BE GENTLE

Little Albert was probably my favorite client. I was working in a residential treatment center for severely troubled children, with my office located on the unit where some of them lived. Albert had been working to control his behavior well enough to earn a weekend pass to be home with his family. He had failed to do so, and I had the unenviable task of breaking the news to him.

We sat down in my office for our chat, and slowly I worked up the courage to break the news. Albert stood up, his cheeks swiftly turning beet red in anger. He headed for the door. I knew his pattern: he would stomp off to his room, destroy something, and guarantee that he was in trouble for the entire weekend.

Stop the action. Think with me for a moment what your immediate response would have been. Most times, I would have reacted something like this:

'Albert, you walk out that door and you'll be confined to your room for the rest of the day.'

'Who cares? I can't go home anyway!' would be his reply.

'You better be careful or you'll really be in trouble. We can make life pretty miserable for you if you don't watch out.'

'It already IS miserable, so tough!' he would conclude, as his routine started. Off to his room, rip up a favorite toy, scream for a while, get the staff angry at him, and then sulk the weekend away. Adult authoritative power meets youthful anger, and loses.

That's not what happened this time. By God's grace, on this particular day my reflexes were different, and I thank God for his control over my words and deeds. As Albert glared at me and headed for my office door (which was closed), I gently slid over and wedged my foot against the door, making it impossible for him to open the door to leave. I asked him calmly, 'Tell me what you're going to do when you leave, and I'll let you go.' He knew better than to answer that question, so he paced and fumed. (He later told me he came close to cleaning my desk off for me, if you know what I mean.) I remained quiet and composed (at least on the outside), and in a few moments Albert's demeanor dramatically transformed from rage into sorrow before my eyes. His eyes moistened, and he collapsed into my arms in tears. I was able to comfort him in his sadness (which was hidden by his anger), preventing his self-sabotage and leading to a weekend of his participating in activities with staff and friends rather than being exiled to his room for destructive behavior. Sure, I had authority to threaten and punish him. But gentleness won the day, and the heart of my young client.

Please don't misunderstand me. Do I believe children should be punished for doing wrong? Absolutely. I even stress this is my previous book, *Of Such is the Kingdom*. But the point I want to make with this story is that our culture, and even our nature, predisposes us to respond to anger with power, strength, or authority. I easily could have engaged Albert in a power struggle. But that was not what he needed. Anger is most often a thin veil for hurt, and Albert was hurt by his failure and loss. By my sensing this and responding in gentleness, Albert received what he really needed—nurture.

This was the way of Jesus. When the woman caught in adultery was brought to him, he didn't chew her out or lecture her accusers. He simply and quietly said, 'Let him who is without sin among you be the first to throw a stone at her,' (John 8: 7). We can see this in his frequent patience with the bickering and power-hungry disciples, his serenity when arrested, and his compassion toward those who crucified him. In our day, we are taught our rights and powers, and that we should use them whenever possible. We need to think seriously about why gentleness, not assertiveness, is a fruit of the Spirit, and how we are to minister to our children in light of this.

Let us first consider how alien gentleness is to our culture and consider some of the roots of our violent and power-oriented age. We'll then look more closely at what the Bible teaches on the subject of gentleness and inquire about how to apply this to our lives and to cultivating gentleness in the hearts of the children we love.

Only the Strong Survive

Ours is not a gentle time. Most men are not 'gentlemen', and increasingly, women are not so gentle, either. Rather, asserting oneself and responding to problems by demonstrating one's strength and power are the socially endorsed methods of coping with this 'dog eat dog' world. Let us look at this again through the window of the media.

TELEVISION

We know television has violence in it, but do we realize exactly how much?

Much like the frog in the kettle, we've become so accustomed to it that we may not notice. Let's look at a sample of the many troubling statistics available.[1] Some 61% of television programs contain violence, and nearly half of these violent scenes contain humor (recall even the more 'innocent' cartoons of long ago, like Tom and Jerry and the Road Runner, had us laughing at the pain of others.) Some 44% of violent scenes portray the perpetrator as attractive and thus more likely to be emulated. Given the time children spend watching television, the average child witnesses 200,000 acts of violence, including some 40,000 murders, when he reaches age eighteen. It is startling that only 4% of violent programs emphasize a non-violent theme, suggesting the overwhelming majority of these programs implicitly, if not explicitly, endorse violence. We know this is bad, with 73% of Americans believing violent television and movies contribute to juvenile crime, remarkably lower than the 80% of Hollywood executives who realize this. Over 1,000 studies have looked at the impact of violence in television and movies, and conclude with no doubt that children who watch significant amounts of violence exhibit more aggressive behavior and attitudes, with the impact being greatest on younger children who are more impressionable and less equipped to discern the motives for the violence.

What leads to the increase of violent behavior in children? Seeing violence with such frequency leads children to see the world as more violent than it really is and to expect and fear violence more than is justified. It desensitizes children to the effects of violence and to its victims. Possibly, though, the most insidious effect is that it leaves children believing violence is the proper way to settle conflicts, leaving no place for God to intervene. Here most of all is where the biblical message of gentleness must be announced.

MOVIES

The line between television viewing and watching movies has blurred as so many movies are shown on television with surprisingly little editing. Theatre favorites are purchased and watched over and over and over in DVD or video format with increasingly graphic realism as technology improves home theatre capabilities.

But this still does not compare to the splendor of the big screen and the powerful audio systems supporting it. The virtual reality of this experience enhances the impact of violence as ever-more-graphic special effects make more horrific acts of violence available to the movie-goer. The more convincing these visual images and sound effects become, the more confusing they are to children (and adults) who witness them. One of the more troubling aspects of my counseling practice is that increasingly I have six and seven-year-old children telling me how their parents allow them to view violent horror movies. How is this excused? Because the children ask to see them and the parents want to be loved by the child, so they acquiesce.

Even worse, often fathers think this is 'good' for little boys so they can be toughened for the real world. (How watching people being beheaded or disemboweled helps prepare for the real world escapes me.)

We frequently have a cavalier attitude toward violence in movies as well. As I write, yet another episode of the never-ending James Bond movie series has come out. Bond must have killed thousands of nameless henchmen by now, many in ways that are intended to make us laugh. It is especially torturous for young children to decode good and evil when the 'good guys' revel in violence in achieving their ends. *The Terminator* and its ilk are even more graphic in portraying heroes being violent. We nonchalantly watch this to the complete exclusion of a godward dimension in these programs and movies. None teach that there is a God in heaven who will do justice on the earth and to whom we appeal in distress. No, we are left to our own resources, and the message is that brute force alone will conquer violence.

Movies (and television programs) are increasingly sexual, gradually introducing portrayals of perversions to further desensitize us to sexual deviance. But I want to draw attention to one particular change that is especially troubling, and that is the increase in the violence (operating often under the euphemism of 'passion') in sexually charged scenes. I recently watched a rerun of a 1960's television program which had a kiss in it. I was struck by the gentle, romantic, caring 'feel' to the scene. Compare this to the 'passionate' portrayals of sex now that are more about selfish passion and self-gratification than about love and caring for the person you are embracing. Sex is portrayed as 'rough' and intense, even violent. Mary Pipher, in her fascinating study of the effects of society on girls, *Reviving Ophelia*, effectively makes this point. Even kisses are hard and intense, not gentle and loving. Women are portrayed as sexual aggressors, fueling the male myth that even when a woman says no, she really does 'want it'. Fight scenes between men and women are common now, with beautiful women going toe-to-toe with men in physical assault, making even a brawl have intense sexual overtones and further blurring the boundary between sex and violence. Sex looks more like rape than an act of love in the movies of our day, a foolish move that promotes the prowling and attacking of the growing band of sexual predators.

The blending of sex and violence is also rife in popular music, with rap and hip hop being the gravest offenders. Most of us have read some of these graphic and nauseating lyrics, and I will not share any examples here. Let it suffice to say that these artists seem to challenge one another to produce the crudest and most explicit words and images they can, debasing women as they go. Gone are songs of love and gentle affection (the Beatles' 'I Wanna Hold Your Hand' is absolutely prehistoric in its innocence now). 'In' are depictions of animalistic drives, group sex, rape, demeaning of the partner, and unbridled doing whatever you feel with no thought for the other person(s). Sexuality, it appears, is man's freedom to assert power over a woman. Music videos provide visual images to support the sexualized messages of the music. Why do we seem shocked by the rates of sexual behavior among young people and sexual crimes including date rape?

But much popular music is of a more purely violent type, and here heavy metal music takes the prize, though rap still runs a close second. Less has been written about the more recent 'emo' music, but it seems likely that its high emotionality, anguish, and pain put it in this category also. In an analysis of heavy metal lyrics by Jeffrey Jensen Arnett[2], violence was the most common theme, and the band Slayer was the worst. Anger and defiance of authorities fills this music. Peter G. Christenson has found that heavy metal listeners are the most extensively studied group. He discovered:

> A preference for heavy metal music is associated with
> a variety of troublesome attitudes and behaviors, including
> drunk driving, casual sex, experimentation with marijuana
> and cocaine, conflict with parents and school authorities,
> anti-establishment attitudes, permissive sexual attitudes,
> Satanic beliefs, and low levels of trust in others.[3]

And the music clearly supports the message as one need only listen to it to feel the hate and anger, regardless of the lyrics.

156

This point is extremely important for Christian parents. In a supposed effort to make the gospel 'relevant' to teens, almost every form of popular music has spawned a contemporary Christian music clone, minus the offensive lyrics. Yet, research shows Christian heavy metal listeners are affected by the music in the same ways as those who listen to the secular versions, with it adversely affecting attitudes toward sex and violence.[4] It enhances young people's acceptance of rude, defiant, and aggressive behavior. In the next few days, my home town is hosting a contemporary music concert with several artists, and is interestingly dubbed the 'Winter Wonder Slam', an aggressive term that I initially thought was for a wrestling match until I looked more closely at the advertisement. Anyone who has been taught that the message of music is only in the words should take notice. The musical style and even the concert names say more. This has broader implications for Christian adaptation of popular music styles, but I leave it to the reader to think and pray that through on her own.

This is not to exonerate other forms of popular music, for country, pop, rock, and other genres have contributed to the rebellious attitudes of children and young people regarding violence and sexuality. I do, however, wish to challenge parents to consider the impact of the music their children admire, giving thought to both the sound qualities and the lyrics. I fear there's not much gentleness to be found out there.

VIDEO GAMES

These modern day 'necessities' for children seem particularly attractive to boys, and these, too, push the limits of our patience with their ever-increasing level of violence. More realistic graphics only make the violence players see and contribute to more scandalous. The point where video games part company with television and movies is that the player is perpetrating the violent acts in the games rather than passively viewing them. I remember an article from *Christianity Today* some years ago which talked about the common problem in soldiers where they could not shoot another person when face-to-face with the enemy. (This reminds me of the famous image from Tiananmen Square years ago when a lone protester stood in front of a line of tanks and stopped their progress. Trained gunners had no trouble shooting into a crowd, but were stopped by a single human face.) The solution, according to this article, is to have soldiers play video games where they shoot at human figures and so desensitize themselves from the natural hesitancy to harm another person.

Recent research confirms the 'wisdom' in this strategy. Exposure to violent video games is highly predictive of future aggressive behavior in children. How strong is this association? It is stronger than the impact of smoking tobacco on lung cancer, stronger than the effect of calcium intake on bone mass, and even greater that the effect of homework on academic achievement. Let me make sure the point is not lost in the statistics: It is more likely that children's playing violent video games will make them violent than doing homework will help their school performance!

Surveys tell us that 60–90% of the most popular video games have violent themes while 59% of fourth grade girls (about 9 to 10 years old) and 73% of boys in that grade say their favorite games are violent. The infamous boys who killed their classmates and themselves at Columbine High School in Colorado some years ago enjoyed the bloody video game Doom and other young people who have shot children at their schools habitually played similar games.

If that were not troubling enough, consider that 90% of teenagers report that their parents never check the ratings of video games they purchase, and only 1% report a parent ever stopping them from purchasing a game based on its rating. It gets even worse. Only 11% of teenagers report parents ever limiting their playing time of video games. In my work, I have seen how some children will hold their parents virtually hostage to retain access to such games, and even parents who might want to control this behavior often face an arduous struggle to do so.

Of course, the best strategy is to teach children that there are many other forms of entertainment besides video games and prevent the problem in the first place. Yet, we must appreciate the powerful addiction that these games can bring to children and be supportive to parents who are struggling to gain some control of their children's video game playing.

Power and Postmoderism

We've worked over the idea of postmodernism pretty well by now, but there is one point we need to make here as we think about gentleness. Postmodern thinking does not allow for truth and encourages skepticism about those in authority. Might is right since we have no way of determining it otherwise. We have no God to do justice in the world, and the lack of truth makes the idea of justice and fairness irrelevant anyway. This moves to the masses in the idea that we have to look out for 'number one', meaning ourselves. We need to assert our own power to avoid being trampled by others doing the same thing. Gentleness will get you nowhere except shoved to the sidelines of life.

Life, then, is about power for most people in our day. Why get an education? Because 'knowledge is power' and gives you an edge over someone else. How do you get ahead in life? By asserting yourself and taking control of your destiny (for power and control are much the same thing). How do we view others? As threats to our personal pursuit of power at worst; as irrelevant to our lives at best. Either way, they are not to keep us from what we want. This is interestingly rather Darwinian as well—the survival of the fittest means we must overcome the less fit to prove our right to survive.

So, boys are to be aggressive. This is greatly tolerated and attributed to their nature. It is good, because gentle boys won't make it in life and so boys need to be toughened up to increase their chances of surviving in the cruel world. Aggressive sports, bullying, and stepping on others' toes are all means to the end of producing a young man who will make it.

Feminism has encouraged much the same approach to raising girls. More and more girls take marshal arts classes, and the cruelty of girls to other girls has led to a spate of books on the subject in recent years. Theirs is often a more subtle meanness, capitalizing on their greater social skills and perceptiveness to hurt other girls emotionally and socially more than just physically. The gentle lass of days gone by has been lost to the assertive, go get 'em young women of today. Don't depend on some man to take care of you; skepticism says you must take control of your own life.

One of the most disturbing of all modern trends is that the church of Jesus Christ has adopted these attitudes as well, accepting the atheistic philosophy that underlies them. We want to use the 'power' of the media to proclaim the gospel; we use the 'power' of business management techniques to grow the church; we 'sell' the power of God to help people reach their power-oriented goals. Weakness has no place in the church either. Churches compete for survival in a competition that is blatantly Darwinian. If the church down the street gets a new sound system, ours must get a high definition projector for the images to support the pastor's talks (not sermons).

How do we reach youth? By power methods of music (have you noticed the volume in churches going up lately?), slick advertising and promotion, and nifty activities. We seek to meet the needs of power-hungry young people and not to appeal gently to them while trusting in the power of our Almighty God.

The most basic problem in all of this thinking is it omits God, both within and outside the church. We buy the idea that might is right but forget there is One who holds all might and has promised to make all things right. Christian gentleness is built on our freedom to rest in the promises of our God as we trust him to take care of things. We are children of the Almighty, so we need not assert our own power. Indeed, to do so is to undermine his ways. Let us consider how this works as we turn to God's Word for guidance.

Gentleness in the Bible

Only with a firm grasp of what Scripture teaches about gentleness will we be able to see how vital gentleness is and how it contrasts with the aggression of our times. The concepts of gentleness and meekness are related in the Greek, so our consideration includes the idea of meekness as seen in the Sermon on the Mount in Matthew 5. In general, the Greek terms suggest that gentleness and meekness are particularly virtuous when one has power but does not assert it. This is the case with Jesus, who exhorted us to take his yoke upon us because he is 'gentle and lowly in heart' (Matt. 11: 29). Paul also alludes to the gentleness of Christ as a basis of his appeal to the Corinthians (2 Cor. 10: 1). Jesus walked the earth as all-powerful God, yet was characterized by gentleness more than assertion of that power. How many times might we, if given such power, zap our enemies to show them what's right. This was not Jesus' style by any means. When Peter asserted power by cutting off the servant's ear (John 18), Jesus responds not with 'Way to go, Peter. Thanks for taking up for me.' Rather, he repairs the damage done by his disciple and submits to those who had come to arrest him.

Paul followed the example of his Lord, describing his ministry among the Thessalonians as his being 'gentle among [them], like a nursing mother taking care of her own children' (1 Thess. 2: 7; cf. 1 Cor. 4: 21). He teaches that such gentleness should characterize a leader in the church (1 Tim. 3: 3), and Christians in general (Eph. 4: 2; Titus 3: 2), with James adding that our meekness should contrast with anger which we are to avoid (Jas. 1: 21). Moreover, the New Testament stresses that we are to pursue gentleness (1 Tim. 6: 11). Our teaching and correcting should be with gentleness (2 Tim. 2: 25), even when others challenge our faith (1 Pet. 3: 16). This is because gentleness and mercifulness characterize godly wisdom (Jas. 3: 17). A gentle and quiet spirit is particularly becoming to women (1 Pet. 3: 4).

We find these themes in the Old Testament as well. David shows gentleness as king (2 Sam. 3: 39) and sees God's gentleness as a key to his being delivered from his enemies (2 Sam. 22: 36; Ps. 18: 35). We are to be gentle in teaching and speech (Deut. 32: 2; Prov. 15: 4). These may surprise us given our tendency to see God as being more 'violent' in the Old Testament.

Let's catch our breath from this quick survey and consider what we've just learned. First, the freedom to be gentle is grounded in the infinite power of God himself. We need not assert our power because it is infinitesimal compared to God's. In the case of teaching, browbeating is futile; it is the Spirit who will convince others of God's truth. This does not mean we need not make good arguments or teach with conviction, but that we ultimately rest on God's grace to convince our hearers.

Little is needed to see how we are to approach children. Are we to teach them? Absolutely, but in the gentle spirit of Christ.

This is because we are trusting God to change their hearts and behavior. Notice that sequence: hearts then behavior. A major theme of our examination of the fruit is that these are largely heart qualities that reveal themselves in behavior. The Greek terms for gentleness carry this overtone as well: it is a characteristic of the individual before it is manifested in actions. It won't develop by threats and pressure, but by the gentle movements of the Holy Spirit in the heart.

One of our shortcomings as parents and ministers to children is that we try to make technique, power, and pressure do the work of God. We spend more time reading books and articles on 'how to' make our children obey than we do praying for them and seeking God's power to manifest itself in their lives. Again, the frailty of our faith is exposed. When we have greater faith in God's power, we more naturally show gentleness.

I would add a word here also about disciplining children. Notice that the Bible teaches even correction is to be done with gentleness. When we spank or correct out of anger, we lose sight of what we are doing. It reveals our personal aggravation and a lack of confidence in God. It should pain us to have to punish our children, and they should see that. When we discipline while angry, the child sees that the wrong was to offend us, not to have disobeyed God. It then confuses a punishment for wrong behavior with a threat to the parent-child relationship. God disciplines his children, but never is unloving. We are to treat our children in the same way.

Gentleness Comes from Seeing Our Weakness

Our biblical survey can be summarized by saying that we are to be characterized by gentleness because we trust that the Almighty God champions our cause. He is the One who has promised to his children to make all things work together for good (Rom. 8: 28), and has all the power necessary to do so. As God by his Spirit teaches us to trust in this, we bear the fruit of that Spirit in gentleness of heart and action. This runs radically contrary to the thought of our day. As we noted earlier, given the loss of belief in absolute truth, most believe that only power itself can force change in the world. This is the case at a national level, at the academic level, and most definitely at the economic level. But we are concerned with the personal level. The culture instructs us through public education, the media, and popular and scholarly writings that we must stand up for ourselves in order not to be trampled under by others, whether this be in our efforts to improve our economic status, our standing in the office hierarchy, on the sports team, or in getting the treatment 'deserved' from a school teacher.

There is great irony in this if we reflect on it. Exactly how is the average person to have personal power to impact the powerful establishment of government, industry, and culture? It is all one has in postmodern thinking, yet it is very little. The honest outcome of this line of reasoning is despair. A few acknowledge this, but most prefer to keep busy and live as though they can make something of life by asserting their power in the world. Thus, people are quicker to cut in front in a queue, speed past us in traffic, or cheat on a test to get an advantage. It is a futile, hopeless way of life that leads only to more irritability. As we observed earlier, our churches often follow this same strategy, becoming larger in number but weaker in spiritual influence.

This contrasts with the wonderful Christian teachings on weakness. We must first face that we are indeed weak. The popular mantra 'You can be anything you want to be' is malarkey, and we know it if we're honest with ourselves. Yet we then teach it to our children. No, we can't be anything we want to be. But 'I can do all things through him who strengthens me' (Phil. 4: 13), all things that God calls us to do. But the key is that we do this in his power, not our own. When we accept the culture's teaching, we try to use our impotence to accomplish not only goals that may run contrary to God's purposes, but even to try to accomplish his purposes. In so doing, we teach our children to do the same.

I know of no one who has written more powerfully on weakness than Marva Dawn[5], a woman whose life testifies to what she teaches on the subject. She reviews the extensive theme of our weakness in Scripture. I remember the first time I read this I was shocked by how pervasive this doctrine is in Scripture. Dr. Dawn then argues that it is precisely in weakness that God 'tabernacles', or makes his presence known. This is vital to the gospel, for until we concede our helplessness to do anything about our sin, we fail to see our need for the Savior.

In Dawn's words, 'Dying to the law, dying to our selves, dying to our attempts to use our own power to accomplish God's purposes are all part of the gospel of grace—the end of ourselves and therefore the possibilities of new life with Christ' (p. 45). She supports this point with Paul's stress on the importance of seeing our weakness as he wrote to the Corinthians, and then shows how common this theme is throughout the New Testament. Her conclusion? 'There is something seriously wrong with our lives and churches [and I would add 'our children'] if we are operating out of strength, rather than the weakness in which God tabernacles' (p. 53).

I am convinced that we struggle with this because we are so overwhelmed by popular views on power and are weak in our faith that God will indeed take care of things. In my own life, I am bewildered by how much easier it is to trust God to forgive my sins than to trust him to defend and provide for me daily. So, I want to fight for my rights, I mentally think of how I might get back at those who have wronged me, and plot how I can prove myself. So, I write from a conflicted heart on this matter. Yet, I am not conflicted about how I ought to think and believe on the matter.

This is a bit abstract, so let me break this down to apply to our concerns for our children to manifest the spiritual fruit of gentleness. We've already observed that this prompts us to challenge worldly thinking about asserting one's own skills to make it in the world, and we saw that using our own raw, emotional power to convince in discipline may lead to problems. Consider now such things as how your child should cope with being teased at school. Do we advocate arguing or even fighting back? Or do we take seriously the hard teachings of Jesus in Matthew 5 on turning the other cheek, going the extra mile, and loving our enemies? These are gentle responses to provocations, but they clearly conflict with our fleshly reflexes. They leave us utterly dependent on the Almighty God to defend us.

Sports are another challenging area to teach gentleness to children. Christians largely advocate for their children to play sports for the obvious benefits of exercise, learning teamwork, and coping with adversity. How do we teach our children to compete while still being gentle? The answers are not simple, but they are important. This is a good topic for a family discussion one evening.

There are more obvious outworkings of what we have learned. I can find no place for violent video games in the lives of children, unless maybe if they are preparing for military service. There is a place in life for entertainment, but with the bountiful options available, I can see no need to choose violent television or movies. I also see no good reason to allow our children to watch media with sassy children in them. It is challenging to turn teenagers away from angry music, though the notion of weakness reminds us that praying for them may be more powerful than preaching to them. Better still is prayerfully to train their musical tastes when younger, bearing in mind that the choice in music betrays something of the character of the individual. That is, there must be some reason such music becomes attractive in the first place.

But gentleness should also be actively cultivated through having our children minister to those who are even weaker, be it the poor, the elderly, missionaries and those with whom they work in impoverished areas. Even teaching children gentleness in how they handle pets and other creatures can help.

The greatest challenge to gentleness is found in coping with adversity. How will your children see you respond to being mistreated by other drivers while in the car or when you do not get the promotion? What will you teach them when they suffer injustices, teasing, and frustrations? Will you point them to their power, or the truth that God will avenge his children and that we would do well to pray for those who do wrong to us?

One last area bearing mention is forgiveness, a concept alien to much modern thought. When we see a nation attacked on the news, we figure a retaliatory attack is coming. That's what we see most often when a person is wronged on television or in the movies. The idea is to get even, or at least see to it that the wrong-doer pays for what they did to us. Yet, as Christians, we know we have spiritual life only because a righteous God has poured his wrath on his only Son so that we might be forgiven of our sins. We need to remember the parable of the unforgiving servant in Matthew 18 and the sobering verse of the Lord's prayer where we ask God to forgive our debts 'as we have forgiven our debtors,' (Matt. 5: 12).

N. T. Wright sees forgiveness as the key lesson to be learned in dealing with the evils of the world.[6] He offers remarkable examples of the Christian testimony of men like Desmond Tutu in responding to prejudice in South Africa, and theologian Miroslav Volf who has written extensively on how he as a Croatian Baptist could forgive his Serbian Orthodox neighbors for the evil perpetrated against his country.

Recall also the moving scene from Victor Hugo's *Les Miserables* when the priest, rather than see to it that Jean Valjean is punished for stealing his silverware, gives him silver candlesticks as well and challenges him to live as a forgiven man. Such images of dealing gently with offense are rare in the media. As those who care for children, we do well to search these out and use them to teach our children.

Yet, no teaching on forgiveness is as powerful as allowing our children to see us forgive employers, family members, neighbors, and strangers in our day-to-day life. Seeing parents, Sunday School teachers, and church leaders as gentle and forgiving is one of the most potent ways of teaching power through weakness to our children.

Albert's weekend was changed from one incident of gentleness, but our relationship was deepened. How great will be the impact in our children's lives of seeing the gentleness of Christ in our lives and in the lives of those in our church families! As we want God to tabernacle in the hearts of our children, let us teach them to be weak, for when we are weak, he is strong (2 Cor. 12: 10). When they grasp this, they no longer must defend themselves with power, but can joyfully demonstrate the gentleness of Christ—just like their parents.

Practical Steps to Gentleness

I urge you prayerfully to reflect on some of the suggestions for promoting gentleness mentioned in the text above. Prayer alone, with your spouse, and with your church is central to children's bearing spiritual fruit. Here are some more ideas to help you put 'feet' to our discussion.

PRESCHOOL CHILDREN

Guide children into more gentle play activities and away from more aggressive forms. Never take the initiative to get them playing video games, and beware advertising that says video games are educational. Horseplay (play wresting and such) can be gentle if you set definite limits to prevent any potentially hurtful or deliberately mean actions.

Choose the media your children consume carefully. There is a huge difference between the rude brashness of *Rugrats*, for example, and the innocence of Charlie Brown and the *Peanuts* characters.

One of the first places forgiveness is learned is with siblings. Intervene early in conflicts among children, and teach them the biblical truths of forgiving.

When young children see people in a movie or television program acting in power-asserting manners, time a moment to point out ways Jesus might have responded.

Fathers especially need to model for children the virtue of gentle-manliness. Your behaviors are reinforced when you back them up with reading stories of gentle men to your children from Scripture and good stories.

ELEMENTARY AGED CHILDREN

It is important at this age for churches to provide gentle role models for children. This means many men need prayerfully to consider working with the children of the church to provide such role models.

Christian biographies can instruct about lives of gentleness. Stories such as that of George Müller can inspire growth in prayer and meekness.

It is vital that we not just complain of violence in the culture, but that we teach children how this is related to our sinful nature and show them how Christian gentleness stems from understanding our weakness.

Strictly monitor all media consumption, and don't feel guilty if you deny them games or programs they want. Again, it is easier to prevent an 'addiction' to media violence than to 'cure' it. Children in middle childhood are still receptive to being steered toward healthier types of play.

Don't merely punish aggressive behavior or language. Ask your child to think of ways they might have responded in gentleness.

TEENAGERS

Though by nature boys will be boys (with the rude and aggressive actions that implies), remember that does not make it right. Our faith robustly teaches that our natural inclinations are not good. So, don't let boys get away with things for this reason.

There is a special meanness in adolescent girls, using social cruelty, hurtful words, and malicious glances as aggression. Christian girls will look as strange as Christian boys when compared to their unbelieving peers. Manners, humility, kindness, and gentleness must be taught as contrasts to the prevailing aggressive images. There are several good books for Christian girls on being a gentle woman, such as Ann Stacy McDonald's *Raising Maidens of Virtue: a Study of Feminine Loveliness for Mothers and Daughters.*[7]

Engage teens is activities that require gentleness. Once again working with older members of the congregation is valuable, or volunteering at a nursing home. Caring for young children in the church's nursery will have similar benefits.

Parents and youth workers should expose the flaws of secular thought to these young persons even as they actively teach the lessons covered in this chapter. Youth leaders in particular should remember the character of God is not achieved by the methods of the world. Youth groups should differ dramatically from other teen social clubs, stressing the gentle character of Christlikeness.

Media can still be restricted at this age, but with increasing difficulty. Focus should shift from legal enforcement of your standards to teaching your teens so they understand your concerns and the dangers of these things. Prayerfully consider why your children might be attracted to violent media and how you might address the root problem in your child's personality and not just set limits.

12

SELF-CONTROL IN A 'JUST DO IT' WORLD

We did it on a whim, but my friend and I set our minds to participating in a canoe race down a stretch of the Mississippi River near Memphis, Tennessee. We were eager and gung-ho, not as young as we felt and oblivious to what was ahead of us.

The race began, and we paddled with great enthusiasm and energy, thinking ourselves rather clever as we scurried out into the powerful river and found the strongest current we could. The next few minutes were thrilling as we paddled, feeling strong as we sped along with the current. We were near the front of the swarm of over one hundred canoes.

The canoes headed for a turn in the course from the Mississippi, upstream into a smaller river which flowed into it. Paddling suddenly became a struggle as we fought the powerful momentum of the water as we crossed it and then turned directly upstream against the flow of the smaller river. We now heaved and sighed with every stroke of our oars as we strained toward the finish line several hundred meters ahead. Now our best efforts seemed to produce little progress toward our goal. We feared we'd be swept out into the Mississippi and continue downstream, so we dug even deeper as our muscles burned and our breathing quickened. From the corner of our eyes we watched the better trained and prepared competitors move past us toward the finish line.

We did make it at last, though exhausted and depleted. Still, we were wiser for the experience. It's easy to feel like you're accomplishing something when everything is headed in the direction you are going, but only when you wrestle against the current do you see your weakness and learn to continue toward your goal against all the pressures to do otherwise. Such is life.

Paul says Christian maturity brings us to where we are no longer swayed by winds and waves of false doctrine (Eph. 4: 14), and as much can be said for our behavior as well. In navigation, it is vital to have a direction, a destination to which you are headed, so that you orient yourself and focus your energies toward it, fighting off the natural forces that would divert and distract you. If we lack a clear destination, we are left to be carried away by the forces around us. As my friend and I learned, we become deceived by the ease of going with the flow and do not know the importance of self-control until we look to a goal that requires us to go against the flow of the world around us. A major goal of the book has been to orient Christian parents to the goal of godliness for our children as exemplified by the fruit of the Spirit, and to warn of the currents that would carry our offspring away.

The metaphor breaks down when we bear in mind that the fruit and the self-control to strive toward them are all gifts of God's Spirit and not things we generate in ourselves and our children. Nonetheless, it is critical that we consider our situation. We are in a culture whose current is mightier than that of the Mississippi, and will carry us and our children along with it if we do not take care. My friend and I, had we not fought the flow, would have eventually drifted into the Gulf of Mexico, far away from the finish line. This holds true for our children, too: we must orient them to the true goals of the Christian faith, and provide training and tools to promote self-control to reach these goals, even as we know it is God working through us to work this spiritual grace in them. Otherwise, they may drift far away from the fold of God.

As we think through these matters, we will look at some ways culture causes our children to drift and consider some results this produces. We will then consider the biblical mandates on self-control and reflect on ways to encourage our children to fight the current that leads them astray.

Current Currents

Psychological research is discovering that self-control (often termed self-regulation in their journals) is quite important and that a lack of it causes problems. This research sees self-control as a person's ability to adjust and focus one's behavior to progress toward a specific goal. While psychological research does not consider that children should be oriented to God, it does maintain that each person has goals and must regulate her behavior toward those goals, fighting off internal and external distractions from these goals. This is exemplified by the popular fitness motto, 'No pain no gain.' We know that we must resist temptations for naughty foods and discipline ourselves to uncomfortable exercise if we are to achieve fitness goals. Educational goals are similar: our children must turn off the television and sit through endless homework sessions to secure a quality education. Despite this awareness of the problem in secular circles, popular culture pushes against higher goals (not to mention Christian ones) like a tsunami onto the coastline. Let us look at some of the ways this happens.

INSTANT GRATIFICATION

We saw in Chapter 7 how modern comforts threaten the fruit of patience, and the same is true for self-control. In an affluent society, children have few opportunities to deal with frustration. If they want something, they are likely to get it. I write this during the Christmas season, and I have heard from many children with whom I work what they are wanting for Christmas and that they are fully expecting to get what they want. No single, simple toy is the object of hope, but expensive video game systems and other pricey electronic gadgets lead the list. There is little wishing or striving involved for these children: their desire is as good as a contract to have.

This trend holds true in numerous other areas. Children place dinner orders at home as if they were in a restaurant, or refuse to eat if it is not something they want. Parents often surrender to this blackmail for fear their children won't eat, or will have their self-esteem damaged if denied. Activities, snacks, privileges, you name it, and children usually get it. And without much waiting for it, I might add. Rarely do children have impulses that are not met with almost immediate gratification. Parents and caregivers have the resources and either seek to make the child 'happy' by satisfying their whims, or to protect them from bad feelings if deprived of their desires.

There are several major problems with this. First, it causes much of the epidemic of angry children we see around us. Accustomed to having their way, they've learned little tolerance for any who would deny them. These children also fail to develop proper self-esteem, for it is rooted in one's sense that one can face a challenge and (with God's grace) meet it. When they never face a challenge and depend on others to solve their problems, they become passive and lack the skills or even the desire to work in order to achieve a goal. Combine this with the passivity created by excessive exposure to the media, and we have serious concerns for our children.

ADVERTISING AND THE LACK OF SELF-CONTROL

We've all seen those commercials: call within the next fifteen minutes to order the product, and you'll receive such and such a bonus. We realize this panders to impulse buying as the seller knows you are trained to be impulsive, lacking in self-control. After all, all advertising wants to decrease our self-control so we'll buy their product which, in almost every case, we don't need. If we needed it, we wouldn't require the extra pressure to get it. Our children are raised on ever-more clever and persuasive advertisements aimed mercilessly at their fallen desires and impulses. When parents conspire to reward the resultant desires in our children, we actively work against the foundations of self-control, the ability to give up the immediate in service to greater goals. We contribute to a world that actively discourages self-control as bad for the economy, not to mention that this causes us to teach our children to indulge themselves while ignoring the grave needs of children in many other parts of the world. It is no surprise that children who watch a lot of television want more of the toys seen in the ads and eat more advertised food than those who watch less. Children now spend or influence 500 billion dollars' worth of purchases each year.

There is little way to keep children away from advertising, for it is everywhere we go. Rather, as concerned adults, we must train our children from early on that constant, immediate gratification isn't good for us as the ads claim. I once heard a childcare expert offer the wise advice that we should tell our children 'no' once a day at least, just to keep them used to hearing it.

VIDEO IMAGES AND THE CONTROLLED SELF

The power of the images of video screens is awesome (in the true sense of the word). The content of what our children view merits plenty of concern, but the process of watching is also most worrisome. The visual stimuli are engrossing, with images on the television changing every five or six seconds either due to a camera change or shift to a new scene. This produces a constant need for the brain to adjust and discourages continuity of thought. Thus, the brain is trained to react in response to rapid stimuli, depriving it of the opportunity to learn to sustain a train of thought or reasoning. Compare, then, the quick responses required in video games to the careful reasoning needed to make a move in chess. Video images train young brains into instant gratification and away from sustained thought. Video is simply not equipped to develop minds that can ponder the world carefully, much less ponder the Creator of the world. Even educational and Christian programs are guilty when they use media that may undermine the message in this way. Reading, outdoor play, and free play with toys you actually handle and move are healthy in more ways than one as each requires sustained attention and thus trains in self-control.

When we read these things, it is easy to think of the current issue of Attention Deficit/Hyperactivity Disorder. Millions of children, especially in the US, are medicated to treat this neurological problem. While I do believe this is a legitimate disorder, I also am sure that television and video programming are failing our children by not training them to control their brains so they can sustain attention to the written and spoken word. Rather, these train them to react to rapid stimulation and to act on impulse.

The nature of this stimulation makes video and computer games actually addictive. The National Institute on Media and the Family describe symptoms of such an addiction as a child spending most non-school hours on these games, falling asleep at school, falling behind in assignments, worsening grades, lying about their game use, choosing these games over time with friends, and being irritable when not playing the games. The problem of addiction, as noted as early as Saint Augustine, is that one becomes enslaved to something that began as a choice. Such slavery is absolutely contrary to self-control. Even if a child does not fit this pattern of addiction, how dependent are our children on media for entertainment, be their interests television, music, movies, or video games? To that extent, our children are hindered in the grace of self-control.

THE TRANSGRESSIVE CULTURE

This is a term drawn from the work of Philip Rieff and described in Jeffrey Jenson Arnett's 'Music at the Edge'. Rieff sees the transgressive as something that violates the prohibitions and commands that keep a society healthy. In the West, these standards have historically been drawn largely from the Christian tradition. But in a transgressive culture, acts of transgression become virtue so that breaking rules is valued over keeping them. How well this describes the changes in culture lately! No longer is it 'cool' to obey the rules and do what you ought to do. Being 'cool' requires pushing the envelope of what is acceptable and this is most often accomplished by showing less and less self-control. We see this in all aspects of the youth culture and have discussed this in various ways throughout this book. Music pushes cruder and cruder language, movies ever more explicit violence, and video games increasingly cruel forms of aggression, and all advocate a reckless defiance of authority in pursuit of one's rights and wishes, giving no place to regulating one's behavior. Drinking has become commonplace among youth, with British youth (according to a report on Radio 1) leading the way among

European nations in teenage drinking and legal problems. In the youth culture, it is now good to be bad. Still, maybe no area shows the transgressive culture like sexual behavior.

UNCONTROLLED SEXUALITY

Let me illustrate this with the news just for the past two or three weeks as I write this late in 2006. A pop star made major headlines as she partied for several nights in a row, drinking heavily and freely allowing photographers to snap pictures of her private areas where she had brazenly worn no underwear—this just weeks after she gave birth to a child! This week, Miss America garnered quite a bit of publicity for her own substance abuse problems and sexual behaviors, allegedly having girl-on-girl kissing sessions with Miss Teen USA. Another beauty queen had pictures published of her kissing other girls very crudely along with shots of her exposing herself in ways that should never represent any civilized state. All of these women are supposed to be role models for younger girls, but seem to be modeling that it is 'cool' to transgress sexual standards rather than uphold them. I choose female examples because we are more accustomed to men pushing sexual boundaries, but now women have achieved equality in transgressiveness. Do what you feel or want with no thought of self-control.

This is the message our children are receiving, and it is one echoed in the media we have already considered. Television permits more explicit sexual behavior and innuendo, with gay and lesbian characters becoming commonplace in programs. Cable television has dedicated several entire series to promoting homosexuality. Teenagers in particular are drawn to shows portraying sexuality, and producers have obliged these tendencies by providing a generous dose of sexual situations in programs watched by youth. Teen movies assume kids are obsessed with sex, and gladly push back boundaries to portray it in more perverted and offensive ways. Then, our schools teach our children that all of this is just fine so long as your partner is willing and you are careful not to catch a sexually transmitted disease.

How does this affect teenage behavior? Though there has been a slight downward trend in the number of teenagers having sex, still 47% of American children in high school report having had intercourse, with 14% reporting having sex with four or more different partners. At this point the US teens are more sexually active than most European countries, but by the age of 20, Great Britain reports just over 80% of young people to have had premarital sex, moving slightly ahead of the Americans. In a report I saw on Fox News this week, up to 95% of Americans report having had sex premaritally. Even those teens that do not have intercourse push the limits. Of the American high school-aged teens that had not had intercourse, nearly a quarter of them had had oral sex. Thinking of the impact of the transgressive, consider that a startling 11% of teens have had anal sex while about one fourth of teens who have sex do so while under the influence of alcohol or drugs.

The stream of sexual transgressive has a fearfully strong current as every aspect of popular culture teams up to draw our children into early, frequent, and even perverse sexuality. The frankness of sexual discussion among teens adds to the ease of drifting into sexual behavior as well. In some groups, teens talk freely on being on their periods, give nicknames to each person's sexual organs, and detail sexual exploits and fantasies. These trends are moving downward as younger and younger children are sexually aware and as younger girls are encouraged to wear sexy, revealing clothing. We pray that our children grow to depend on God for strength to paddle assertively against this rushing river of uncontrolled sexual urges.

PEOPLE AND THE PROBLEM

The media is not the only culprit. Culture is a composite of individuals, and increasing the power on our microscope allows us to see more clearly some of the types of people who pull our children downstream.

First and foremost are peers. It is a truism of life that peers are more likely to influence toward negative behavior than toward positive behavior, toward sin more than toward righteousness. As children grow into teenagers, the influence of peers increases. This is not necessarily bad. Part of the process of separating from parents to become adults involves finding a place in the broader social world, namely among friends. Much of the uncontrolled behavior we have discussed is driven by young people's need to fit in, be accepted, and not to feel ostracized. It is fascinating how universal is the denial of teens that peers pressure them, for there is no doubt that they do. Christian teens need not only to fight against the pressures of peers, but need positive peer pressure from Christian friends to follow our Lord.

Here is where church youth groups serve a vital function. They afford a place for Christian young people to be around others who are seeking God above all, and to be encouraged in that pursuit. They afford leaders who model the godliness they pursue, and an intergenerational context to help keep their bearings on their spiritual goals by knowing others further down the path of godliness. Yet, many church youth groups seek merely to mirror the ways of the world by adapting so much to the culture that the message is lost. They think that by being in the middle of the stream they will attract more children and teenagers. The music seeks to be 'relevant' and the activities entertaining. Church youth need to have fun together, but they still must huddle together to gain strength to stand against the pressures of the world around them. They are to encourage one another toward self-control and away from self-indulgence. If our churches fail in this, we have become part of the problem rather than part of the solution.

The same holds true for parents. We have already seen how easy it is for Christian parents to mimic the world in what they want for their children and how they raise them. If we are in the middle of the stream of godless culture, it is hard to encourage the self-control needed to steer them out of it. We must eschew worldliness and be examples of lives lived intentionally for the glory of God, demonstrating self-control in what we do at work, at home, and in the community. Neil Postman powerfully describes this as 'conceiving of parenting as an act of rebellion against…culture.' Our children need rebellious parents in Postman's sense.

FINDING POLARIS

Our postmodern world offers our children no vision of what they should become, other than consumers and people who do whatever they feel. This does not resonate with the image of God in which we are created, yet it is all the world has to offer. Our culture provides no goal toward which children should strive, leaving them to drift along blindly with the currents that flow away from God. Occasionally we see examples of those who fight against the flow. For example, some children will sacrifice entertainments and even friends to pursue a sport or to master a musical interest. But most children of our day grow to be rather aimless and even cynical. There is no guiding star to direct them, so they drift with the current.

Sociologist James Davison Hunter observes that children are to have character, a forming of the moral personality around one's deepest beliefs. 'Character is formed in relation to convictions and is manifested in the capacity to abide by those convictions even in, especially in, the face of temptation.'[8] In our day, most children do not have convictions, and so have little reason to stand against temptation.

This speaks to the critical issue that Christians who care about children must face. We must point them to the Polaris of Christlikeness, to seeking first his Kingdom (Matt. 5: 16) as the central conviction of their lives. It is not enough to teach them to say no to sex and drugs, for temptations will easily overpower them without character formed by convictions. We must cast a vision for following Christ in positive ways so they can persevere in self-control as they pursue this goal, even going across or against the prevailing currents of our time. It is this fruit of self-control that then strengthens them to stand against the works of the flesh that Paul lists earlier in Galatians 5 that would deter them from godliness. This begins with parents seeing the critical need to go against the flow. To do this, we do well to better understand the Bible's teachings on self-control.

Self-Control in the Bible

In Galatians 5: 23, the Greek translated 'self-control' in modern translations was translated 'temperance' in the King James Version. This evokes images of people controlling their consumption of alcohol, being tempered in how much they drink. The limitations of this image is a primary reason most modern translations have used 'self-control', showing its implications about controlling all aspects of keeping the self in check, not just regarding liquor. Self-control is the Spirit's gracious control of the will to empower it to resist temptation and distraction as it keeps its focus on following Christ. A survey of how the term is used will help us better understand its implications for raising children.

Scripture echoes the idea of the athlete's self-discipline in pursuit of excellence, as mentioned above. Paul notes in 1 Corinthians 9: 25 that an athlete exercises self-control in all things, but only to win a perishable wreath as prize. Consider that an athlete has to eat well, get enough sleep, work out diligently, and avoid bad habits that might hinder his performance. Paul challenges us to the same type of self-control, but toward an imperishable reward. Two verses later the apostle confesses how he disciplines his body to keep it under control, with the Greek being more literally translated 'I pummel my body and make it a slave.' No drifting here; this is very deliberate, intentional self-control to equip Paul for the ministry God has given here.

The will's control over behaviors of the body is very much in focus here, and this is seen elsewhere, particularly with regard to sexual behavior. In 1 Thessalonians 4: 4, Paul challenges us to control our bodies so as to avoid passion and lust and in keeping with 'holiness and honor'. Contrast this with the impulsive, passionate sex endorsed in today's culture. Such passions should be tamed by the will, and the ability to do so is a fruit of the Spirit. 1 Corinthians twice uses the term specifically about sexual behavior, not surprising given the highly charged sexual culture of that city. In 7: 5, married couples are exhorted not to deprive each other of marital pleasures. Why not? Lest Satan exploit their lack of self-control. A few verses later (v. 9) this same logic is given as a reason to marry in the first place. The apostle is keenly aware of the dangers of sexual lust and the need for self-control.

It is worth mentioning that this issue is even more important in our day. With children maturing physically earlier and waiting until they are older to marry, the time between sexual awareness and marriage has grown to be 10 or more years. Combine this with the ubiquity of sexual temptations and the lowered standards for behavior, and we indeed have a crisis demanding the utmost of self-control. This is a very, very big deal and we need to take it most seriously.

It is interesting that the New Testament particularly stresses for women to be self-controlled, with Paul instructing Timothy that women should adorn themselves modestly and with self-control, and that self-control should accompany faith, love, and holiness in their virtues (1 Tim. 2: 9, 15). How, in light of this, can Christian parents buy immodest clothing for our daughters? Titus 2: 5 lists self-control with the womanly virtues of purity, working at home, kindness, and submissiveness to one's husband. This fruit thus manifests itself in a woman's roles in the family, and one might infer this refers to controlling her words and deeds so she does not say or do everything she might feel with respect to her husband and children. This teaching might particularly apply to the reflexive tendency to discipline children in anger and irritability rather than calmly. Self-controlled discipline and correction become a godly mother (and father as well).

Self-control is a fruit that we should see in our leaders. Overseers (elders) are specifically commanded to exhibit this quality (1 Tim. 3: 2; Titus 1: 8). The context of this directive in Titus is concern over rebellious and divisive people ('transgressives'?) who are ruining entire households with false ideas. Our leaders, then, should not only model a life of self-control before our congregations and particularly our children, but warn us of the dangers that threaten us.

Paul then charges Titus to exhort older men (2: 2) and younger ones (2: 6) to be self-controlled. Since these are in addition to the women already mentioned, clearly Paul sees self-control to be pivotal in the life of a healthy church. Peter also stresses the importance of this fruit (1 Pet. 4: 7; 2 Pet. 1: 6).

A lack of self-control is seen as an evil (2 Tim. 3: 3) for it leaves a man vulnerable to all types of invasion from the outside (Prov. 25: 28). It contrasts with fear in 2 Timothy 1: 7 as Paul says God gives us a spirit of power and love and self-control instead. These spiritual gifts of grace equip us to walk with our God, knowing he is faithful to his promises, and God-given self-control will keep us from distractions as we serve in power and love. What then is there to fear? But then again, what does it reveal if we are afraid?

How is self-control obtained? Titus is most instructive in this regard, teaching us that God's grace has appeared, 'training us to renounce ungodliness and worldly passions, and to live self-controlled, upright, and godly lives in the present age' (2: 12). First, notice our explicit dependence on the grace of God. No clever gimmicks or 'how to' advice is offered; rather, we are called to look to God for this gift. So with our children, while we take steps to promote and teach self-control, nothing will be more important than imploring the God of grace to grant self-control to our young ones. Then, consider the deliberate stance against the currents of ungodliness and worldly passion. As we appreciate God's grace more deeply, we decide to stand firm against things that would cause us to drift from our dear Father. This self-control then moves us toward godliness even as my friend and I fought the current to reach the finish line. God's grace make the Christian's struggle less burdensome (Matt. 11: 30).

So what is the goal of the Christian's self-control, the 'finish line' upon which we are focused? Notice verse 13 which tells us, 'waiting for our blessed hope, the appearing of the glory of our great God and Savior Jesus Christ.' We persevere in controlling our inclinations to sin as we anticipate the return of Jesus for which we fervently hope. If we are indeed seeking first God's kingdom, we will naturally push aside the world's cries to follow the masses. Our Polaris is Christ himself, and the hope of being with him, freed from the sin and temptations that plague us today.

The Christian can hardly argue with Paul's vision and exhortations toward this goal, and the need for self-control as we move toward that wonderful day. Yet, we must admit that we struggle to realize this in our own lives, even as adults. What a challenge then to cast this vision for our children! Daunting as the task may be, we follow Christ and look to him for the grace needed. Here are a few general thoughts to stimulate our reflection.

Guiding Our Children to the True Finish Line

Many of us have had the experience of beginning a new exercise routine, be it going to a gymnasium, running, or participating in a sport. Initially, it takes great will power to stop everything else and exercise. As we develop a routine, it is more natural to start our routines and, if all goes well, we eventually even learn to enjoy them. Though this analogy does not work completely given that it omits the work of God in our hearts, it still gives us a basic framework for guiding our children to be amenable to self-control. It may begin with discipline which they resent and resist, but it can lead to routines and practices which are more natural. As their wills and minds come more fully in mind with God, doing the things that honor him will bring joy and not be seen as burdensome.

This must start with parents. We need to take time in prayer to confess our failures and ask God to help us see the ways we are leading our children down the streams of godless culture. Our words will not speak any louder than our lives. Prayer for God's grace is the starting point. Next, it is incumbent upon us consistently to point our children toward the goals of the Christian life. Glorifying God as we anticipate his return is the focus. The stronger grasp our children have of the purpose of their lives, the better equipped they will be to navigate the currents that run contrary to it.

We must expose the dangerous waters around us for what they are. We must eliminate, control, or limit media from early on. We must speak up and challenge godless views of life when we hear them on television or in the movies. Our children must know the things of the world for the threats they are. Just as the fruit was beautiful to behold in the Garden of Eden, our children must learn to challenge their senses and see that what looks or feels good is not necessarily good for them.

Church leaders, youth leaders, and Christian educators must join the effort as well. Churches should challenge and encourage parents in their task. Education has a pivotal role to play as children develop intellectual skills to discern the times. We must cherish each Sunday School hour, each youth group meeting, each Bible study time and worry less about entertaining our children and more about equipping them with the resources for self-control that will be essential if they are to avoid the pitfalls of the world around them. Point them toward the goal, alert them to the dangers, encourage them on the way, and cultivate a subculture among the church's young people that is joyfully transgressive of the transgressive culture around them.

Let us consider a few specifics that might help get us started.

Suggestion for Promoting Self-Control

PRESCHOOL CHILDREN

Young children need open spaces to move about, but set reasonable limits on these and teach them to control their bodies in this most basic way. For example, make them stay in their seats during meals, at home and in public.

It is worth stressing again that parents should limit young children's exposure to advertisements which teach discontent. Self-control is easier when you're not pulled in as many directions.

Give some structure to the day. Establish a thirty minute time each day to read to your child. Schedule a walk together each day. Not only do these build relationships, but they teach young children to conform their behavior to the structure you set and thus encourage self-control.

In devotions, Sunday School classes, and at other opportune moments, teach young children that they live to serve God and develop this focus from the beginning.

Closely monitor your child's behavior around other little ones. Teach self-control in play by correcting selfish or rough play patterns, mean statements, and rude actions. In particular, correct naughty behaviors learned from other children or the media.

ELEMENTARY-AGED CHILDREN

Teach them to do routine chores that require self-control. Make them clean up their messes, take dishes to the sink, put their clothes away, etc. The key is to do these without

185

being prompted, so that their will is more active than when we wear them down by nagging.

Read to them, or have them read, biographies that tell of persons who went against the grain and demonstrated godly self-control. Biblical stories such as that of Daniel and his friends who resisted the king's food, defied orders to worship a false god, and remained faithful in prayer exemplify the fruit of self-control.

Regular times for homework and dinner help teach self-control. A discipline such as learning to play a musical instrument or participating in a sport, and practicing regularly, can help also.

Limit media time. Let children know how long they have each day, and teach them to stick to this.

Keep them focused on the true goals of life. Show them how school fits into serving God well, how the disciplines of daily life bring God glory, and how serving others pleases their Heavenly Father. Even recreation is not an end in itself, but refreshment for soldiers that makes them better prepared for battle.

ADOLESCENTS

Make them increasingly responsible for their own possessions and lives. Give consequences for messy rooms, running late, and having to be reminded to do chores. They need to learn to do these things as a form of discipline, not just because of your external pressure on them.

Teach teens to make schedules so studying and quiet times find a place in their activities. You need not be overly rigid, but teens do well to learn to manage their fun around their responsibilities.

Guide their thinking about colleges, careers, and relationships to conform to the true goals of life, showing how impulsive activities detract from these. Explicit times of discussing these things are important.

Monitor the activities of the church youth group, and encourage the leaders to keep a focus on Christian goals while teaching and encouraging self-control amid the threats of teen culture.

Spend meaningful time with teens to better understand their world and to keep communication lines open. Ask questions that make them think through what they believe and do, resisting the parental temptation to preach. They need to learn self-control in their thinking as well as behavior.

13

THE CHURCH AS COUNTERCULTURE

An upper middle class suburb of the southern US city of Atlanta, Georgia, seems a strange setting for a television profile of a syphilis outbreak among teenagers. America's Public Broadcasting System did just that with Frontline's *The Lost Children of Rockdale County* which weaves the accounts of a number young of people caught up in promiscuous sexuality and its impact on their lives. One theme of the program is how one boy sought to change his life and behavior by becoming involved with a church's youth ministry which primarily consisted of regular concerts by the church's Christian rock band. This boy, and many other teens like him, came to the concerts and 'got religion' for a while. But it didn't stick, and soon he was back to his sinful and transgressive ways.

Ever since I saw this moving documentary, I've been troubled by the way this boy sought out faith at a church which was doing what it thought was right to make the Christian faith 'relevant' to young people. Video of these services showed a crowd of young people enjoying the concerts apparently moved to praise God. So what was wrong?

Over time, I've come to some conclusions. First, I have doubts that simply making music that effectively mimics the secular music of the day does much good. The truth of these lyrics didn't change this boy's life, even if the music did get him into a church building. Second, from what you could tell in the program, adults were not to be found in this outreach. The worship was led by teens and for teens. As throughout the documentary, adults were apparently aloof and distant as these young people struggled. I assume this was not for lack of caring, but due to their belief they might hinder the young people. Finally, there seemed to be no conscious effort to draw these adolescents into the life and ministry of the church. It seemed that just having them in the building made the ministry a success, even if they were not discipled and mentored.[1] In many ways, then, this exposes some of the problems with current ideas of youth ministry. It is well-intended, but I fear it is rather misguided.

If we are to see fruit in the lives of our children, and to see them draw others, including our prodigals, to Christ, we need to consider the implications of what we have discussed for how our churches are ministering to our children and young people. We have made several allusions to the role of the church in cultivating the soil of our children to bear the fruit of the Spirit. As we bring to a close our meditations on keeping our children unstained by the world, let us reflect on the role of the church in supporting our prayers and actions on behalf of these young ones.

Shallow Means to Shallow Ends

Pardon yet another water metaphor, but there is little better way to sum up our current popular culture than to say it is shallow. Indeed, even secular author Todd Gitlin laments that 'despite the occasional thoughtful or beautiful exception, shallowness is the condition of the bulk of popular culture and remains so even if the observer does not sink into a chiding voice.'[2] Culture used to mean the type of arts that required training and 'cultivation' to appreciate. You needed to know what was going on with a symphony to appreciate the genius of the conductor, or to grasp the different artistic styles to admire a painting. But only the ability to tap a toe is requisite to get into popular music, or to sit and stare to be mesmerized by television. Shallow media can only carry a shallow message, one that is easily trivialized as is the art and philosophy of this culture. Yet, the gospel is not shallow in its meaning, and certainly is not trivial.

Consider the consequences of a shallow culture. Children easily move from diversion to diversion because there is no central theme around which to organize their lives, no North Star as we discussed in Chapter 12. They move from experience to experience with little purpose to govern life other than seeking immediate gratification. Theologian David Wells describes children of the postmodern world as

> cut loose from everything, hollowed out, eclectic, patched together from scraps of personality picked up here and there, leery of commitments, empty of all passions except that of sex, devoid of the capacity for commitment, fixated on image rather than substance, operating on the seductive elixir of unrestricted personal preference, and informed only by personal intuition.[3]

If this is the situation created by the culture, why would we think that by adapting the shallow techniques of that culture we will help these children?

Yet that is exactly what many churches are doing as they try to make children and youth ministry so 'cool' that they offer nothing of substance. This trend is described in disheartening detail in Cathy Mickel and Audrey McKeever's timely book, *Spiritual Junk Food: The Dumbing Down of Christian Youth*.[4] They trace the basis of many of the contemporary youth ministry techniques and curricula to their roots in humanistic psychology, explaining their propensity to promote tolerance, self-esteem, relativism, and even personal values in contradiction to the teachings of parents.

As Christians, we must understand and relate to the culture in which our children and teens are living, and we have sought to learn more about it in the preceding pages, but it is most confusing why our church leaders and youth ministers would adapt those very ways to reach youth. My wife was told of one youth minister at a conservative church whose philosophy was to get the kids so amused that when they reared their head in laughter, he might pour a little gospel down their throats.

As in the PBS program described earlier, we may get them in the building this way only to send them away when they see we have nothing to offer to hold their patchwork lives together. Children who grow within a church that focuses on entertainment and trivial techniques may decide their faith is irrelevant or inconsequential, unless their parents have been very intentional in teaching them the ways of God and the importance of spiritual fruit. Parents should do this regardless, but the church should complement these efforts, not undermine them.

Frankly, I believe we seriously underestimate our children and youth. In counseling, I find they think deeply and ask hard questions only to see their parents and church leaders evasive and focused on entertaining them rather than genuinely seeking their spiritual maturity and fruitfulness. The shallow culture leaves a longing in our young people, but our churches are missing it because we're too busy trying to mimic the ways of the world. Even the ministries to adults are becoming more airy, leading to the view of God as being 'weightless' (to borrow David Wells' term), having little impact as the church that uses the world's techniques to impress the world, while failing to grow its members as it is commissioned to do. We must clear our heads and rethink what we are doing. God calls the church to be a different, to be a counterculture, and that should be more evident in this day of increasingly godless culture.

Christian Counterculture

We have spoken much of the dominant position of technology in our culture and thus in the lives of our children. For better or worse, we have technology all around, and it can be friend or foe. Given my penchant for typographical errors, I thank God for the computer on which this is being typed. I recall the messy white-out materials I used for papers while in college, and am glad those days are behind me. We need to understand and use technology in appropriate ways in our churches, yet the medium cannot become the message. Crystal clear speaker systems for our churches are of little use if they are not proclaiming truth, and truth is what the church is about.

THE CHURCH AS COUNTERCULTURE

The truth of God's Word is that we are not to be conformed to the world, but to be transformed by the renewing of our minds (Rom. 12: 2). This verse introduces a section in Romans where Paul outlines the importance of the body of Christ and our unity, a stark contrast to the individualism that marks our culture. True Christians are known by genuine love, hating evil, holding fast to good, showing brotherly affection to believers, being fervent in spirit, patient in tribulation, and constant in prayer, giving and hospitality (Rom. 12: 9–13). How unlike the world! And these qualities resonate with the fruit of the Spirit that we have contemplated.

Our churches should be places where the fruit and other countercultural aspects of Christian character are on display for our children and those around us to see. We must relate to the culture while being different from it. To begin, we should pray and work to be the community that Paul described above, one that attracts by love, not by technique.

We do this by taking our task more seriously as members of the Christian community and parents of children. We must ask more of church members even as we encourage parents to ask more of their children.

> Churches imagine that the less they ask or expect of believers, the more popular they will become and the more contented the worshipers will be. The reverse is true. Those who ask little find that the little they ask is resented or resisted; those who ask much find that they are given much and strengthened by the giving.[5]

The 'more' we must ask is to be countercultural, to be different, to be Christlike, to be spiritually fruitful, and not merely those who bear the name of Christ without bearing his likeness.

This requires us to esteem covenant values over individualism; to value service to one another over a therapeutic gospel that simply stresses that Jesus will make us feel good by meeting our felt needs.[6] One of the biggest dangers in modern psychology (and I say this as a psychologist) has been the individualistic focus. Though some therapists have broadened their scope to include the family, the broader community has been undervalued. Only as psychology has attempted to be sympathetic to differing cultural contexts has it realized that for some (such as many Asian cultures, but also Latino/Latina groups, African-Americans, etc.) sacrificing selfish goals for the community is honored. It is lamentable that some secular cultural traditions have done a good job at preserving communal values while much of the Western church has abandoned them for therapeutic individualism. The irony is that in God's communal model, by bearing one another's burdens we have an entire community to help us, rather than just a 'Jesus and me' approach. The old adage 'It takes a village to raise a child' is correct, but in God's plan, that village is the covenant community of the church.

Even as we have stressed throughout this book how intentionally and passionately we must stand against the 'stains' of our culture, so we must just as intentionally and passionately live for the good of the members of our counterculture and those surrounding it. God does not neglect the individual's emotional needs; he just has a different solution than the world offers. As our churches become communities of godliness, centered on biblical truth, our children will see themselves as welcome members of a culture that serves them magnificently even as they serve it and the God who has called it into being. The fruit of the Spirit are given not just for individual godliness, but to equip us to serve others. One of today's great challenges is to convince our children that, in contrast to the screaming message of the culture, we are here to serve God and others, not ourselves. In God's wisdom, it is exactly in such service that our truest joy abides.

One of the greatest benefits of the church to our children, especially as they mature into adults, is to provide a community to which they belong. Many of young people's 'who am I?' questions can be answered by viewing oneself as a valued and contributing member of the Christian community of the local church, which is in turn part of the Church universal, both around the world and down through the ages. A child's peers in the children's ministry or youth group are an important aspect of this, but the entire congregation and people of God are ultimately in view here. This is one thing the church in our opening vignette missed. They are not alone in so doing.

This means that churches need to find places to make children feel they belong. There are times for children to be segregated from adults (for age-based children's and youth classes outside of worship times). But there must be opportunities for cross-generational fellowship and ministry, where children take their place in the corporate worship of the whole body, not least throughout the services on the Lord's Day. Other groups in the church should also include children and youth so they can see the fruit in the lives of older saints and discover role models beyond their parents. There is a critical need to find opportunities for children and youth to participate actively in church life. Music ministries, service opportunities, ushering, distributing bulletins, welcoming visitors, serving in the nursery, helping in Vacation Bible School, assisting in food preparation, maintaining the building and grounds, and helping the elderly and infirm are only a few ways that young people can feel more a part of the community. In doing so, we both cultivate the fruit of the Spirit and let it nourish the rest of the community.

The church is to be a place where a community of truth is experienced and where the fruit of the Spirit is manifested along with his gifts. It is not to be a place for occasional entertainment, but one where even the youngest child feels he belongs and is loved, and where teenagers are welcomed and cared for. It is to be, in the words of Marva Dawn, a parallel society.[7] That is indeed what God intends the covenant community to be.

Life in the Parallel Society

I am arguing for a righteous conspiracy, where parents, church leadership, church members, and other children collude to exhibit the fruit and other characteristics of Christlikeness so our children are exposed to these everywhere they turn in the community. This affords them the opportunity to experience genuine love and fellowship and to see how marvelously different it is from the shallow, fleeting pleasures of the world. They then simultaneously benefit from the spiritual fruit of the community while being drawn into a desire to manifest the same. To return to the Easter clothing analogy at the beginning of the book, the more they appreciate the beauty of this clothing and sharing it in common with others, the more motivated they are to keep it from being stained by the world. Allow me to close with some suggestions about children in the church.

PASTORS AND CHURCH LEADERS

Shepherds of the flock are to care for every lamb, so children should be a priority in the prayers, deliberations, planning, and action of all church leaders. No one in the church should be more aware of and educated about the dangers of the world than pastors, elders, and deacons. Nor should anyone be more passionate about keeping the flock, including the children, unstained by the world. Yet, often children's and youth ministry is farmed out to others who receive relatively little supervision. It is a good thing for churches that are large enough to have children's and youth ministers, but these should operate under the supervision of the leaders of the entire flock, and should be wise in the things of God, not just trained in educational techniques.

Church leaders do well to consider how well they have thought and prayed through their approaches to caring for children and young people in the church. I will not repeat what I said in *Of Such is the Kingdom* except to reiterate the need to have a clear theology of children and philosophy of ministry built upon it.

One thing my church does that I recommend is to have an elder present in the youth Sunday School class. Not only does this provide a monitor to keep the teachers accountable, but it also exposes the youth to an elder so that they can know him as a model of Christian virtue. We also have the church divided into shepherding groups each guided by an elder, again keeping leadership in touch with the younger lambs.

I also believe that children are greatly impressed when church leaders know them and acknowledge them by name. A pat on the head, handshake, or a word of encouragement can be a potent gesture for children of all ages. An occasional note to each young person that an elder is praying for them can strengthen young people in the battle against the world.

I am suggesting that we focus on 'microministry' and not just on more elaborate programs. I urge each church leader, and leaders in women's ministry as well, to pray for wisdom in how to reach out to the children and teens under your spiritual care, and how to live godly lives before them while equipping them to manifest the Spirit's fruit and avoid the stains of the world.

YOUTH AND CHILDREN'S MINISTERS

First, I thank God for each who has heeded the call to serve in one of these roles. The importance of these roles is often underestimated by our churches, and I want to thank you for your obedience to the call to serving Christ and his Church in this capacity.

Much of this chapter has been written largely for you, and I urge you prayerfully to consider your goals and methods. I cannot tell you precisely how to balance Bible studies with prayer times and fun times in the limited amount of time you have with your charges. Yet, each of these activities should serve your overall goals of nurturing the young plants of the Lord's vineyard and protecting them from the surrounding elements. Do not shoot too low. Remember the *Westminster Shorter Catechism* was written for children, though today even adults find it challenging to learn. The difference is in our expectations. The saints of old believed their children could learn a great deal and live it. We should, too.

Don't fall for the idea that young peole need more time for clean fun (though a solid dose is in order). Rather, challenge them with hard questions and teach them to be critical of the world around them. Encourage them to have a passion for godliness and truth. Involve the parents and pray diligently for all under your care. Balance time spent separate from the larger body of Christ and time with it. Deliberately plan activities to serve the elderly and infirm, the poor and the needy. Alert our little ones to the grave poverty around the world and contrast it with our wealth.[8] Seek God's guidance for at least one community ministry and one world ministry that could become a focus for your children or youth. Have your youth participate in that local ministry, and be active in praying for, raising awareness of, and raising money for a global ministry. (This is especially powerful if the ministry is focused on underprivileged or persecuted children and youth.) All of these are places for the graces of the Spirit to be cultivated and used for others. Meanwhile, guard your own heart as well, for you are to model the fruit of the Spirit for others to see.

PARENTS

Parents are the front line of ministry, and we have covered various things you can do to minister to your children. I would focus for a moment on the fundamental choice of a local church in which to worship, serve, and raise your family. I am not advocating that you change churches if you are members of one already. Rather, if you are seeking God's guidance in finding a church home, whether you are a new believer or have been convicted of your need to belong to a local congregation, do extensive research on each church's approach to ministry to children and youth. Certainly you want a church that is true to Scripture, but you also want one that will work with, and not against, you in protecting your children from the world and teaching them the ways of God.

For readers who have a church home, I ask you to thank God for the positive ways your church supports your efforts to raise fruitful children. But I also exhort you to encourage your church leadership to consider ways they might be more active and intentional in ministering to the children and the youth of the congregation. Pray for these leaders, for the pressures of the world do not steer clear of church leaders, but if anything they are a focus of our demonic foe. Volunteer to help with new initiatives to pray for and minister to children in your congregation. It takes little to complain, but it requires godly courage to offer to help.

I am confident all who name the name of Christ in truth care for the youngest lambs of the flock. Yet in our modern world, it is easy to misunderstand how to care for these little ones, or to be so distracted that we fall short of the gentle spiritual nurture they require in a threatening world. May we commit ourselves to more diligent prayer for and ministry to the children with which God has blessed us.

14

THE MISSING INGREDIENTS

Well, if you've made it this far, there is evidence that you have
one of the fruit of the Spirit, patience. We have covered quite
a bit of territory since we began this journey together. If your
experience in reading this is anything like mine in writing it,
you may feel overwhelmed, discouraged, and distraught—even
more so if you are the parent of a prodigal. Our children face so
many dangers. Even we as adults don't stand against these as we
should. It seems keeping ourselves and our children unstained
by the world is far more challenging than keeping children's
Easter clothes clean. It simply seems impossible.

The dangers are everywhere. Doing what it takes to guard
our children and promote spiritual fruitfulness in their lives
is daunting. Being 'good' parents and raising godly children
seems harder than we had thought. Discouragement
comes easily. Also, as noble as is the vision of the church as
counterculture, it seems distant from the realities of most of
our congregations which are made up of sinful humans like
us. Maybe this whole book seems to have diagnosed a terminal
disease that will take the spiritual lives of our children given
the drastic measures needed for the cure. For some readers,
you are already experiencing the pain of children who have

become stained. For others, you may feel weak in the face of the challenges you anticipate as your children grow.

Then again, maybe this study has challenged and motivated you. You want to change, and to become more intentional in raising your children to manifest fruit and thus stay unstained by the world. Yet how to begin? How are you to sustain the long process of doing these things over a period of years? For all of your motivation, it is difficult to take the first steps.

Let me try to encourage you in all of these concerns. Reading this book may make you more aware of the challenges we face, and maybe even more educated about the fruit of the Spirit in the lives of our children. But it is not intended as a mere intellectual exercise, for writer or reader. It is meant as a call to awareness and to action. Yet we identify with Jesus' disciples, for 'the spirit indeed is willing, but the flesh is weak' (Matt. 26: 41). But recall from our discussion of gentleness that weakness is the route to God's power. To grasp this, there are two important pieces we need to add to complete our study.

Think with me for a moment. If I were to ask you what are the two most important qualities of the Christian life that are not named among the fruit in Galatians 5, what might you answer? This answer struck me as I prepared to write this chapter.

Remember 1 Corinthians 13: 13? Three things abide, and the greatest of these is love, a fruit of the Spirit. The other two? Faith and hope. These are the ingredients needed to complete our recipe.

Faith is fundamental to all of the fruit of the Spirit. If we do not believe in God, and believe that his Son Jesus has died and risen again to save us from our sins, then we will not care about our children's spiritual well-being or that they manifest the fruit of their Spirit in their lives. Yet, it is strange that we have strong faith that God will save us from our sins, but struggle to find faith in his ability to change our daily walk with him, to protect our children from the wiles of the devil, and to work the fruit of the Spirit in their lives. The just are not only saved by faith, but are to live by faith, and faith is God's gift to us. We need not muster up our willpower and determination on our own, exerting resolve to change. We've learned from our New Year's resolutions that such commitments don't last long.

Rather, we look to God in our weakness to supply the faith we lack as we follow him and seek his best for our children.

Faith looks to God and apprehends his power to accomplish his will, giving us hope. But we may not grasp the fullness of this. Sure, we hope we grow spiritually. We hope our children will be unstained. We hope they will be spiritually faithful and fruitful. We hope our churches will support and encourage us in the task of raising them. But this hope is not necessarily hope in the biblical sense for, if we are honest, these are things for which we wish more than hope. Biblical hope is wrapped in faith that the thing hoped for is going to happen for certain. For example, Titus 2: 13 speaks of the blessed hope we have of the 'appearing of the glory of our great God and Savior Jesus Christ.' Paul is not wishing for Christ to return as he wonders whether or not he will. He knows by faith that this hope is certain, for 'faith is the assurance of things hoped for' (Heb. 11: 1).

Similarly, we do not rejoice in wishes for they are uncertain, but we rejoice in hope (Rom. 12: 12). Such hope is from the Holy Spirit (Rom. 15: 13), even though it is not listed among the Spirit's fruits. How does the Spirit mete this out?

The first verses of Romans 5 show one way. Our faith, given to us by God, gives us access to God's grace. Knowing God's grace in our lives causes us to rejoice in the hope of God's glory. After all, if he can indeed save us from our sin, he must be glorious. God's glory is seen more fully when, through hardships and sufferings, we develop endurance, then character, then hope. Faith and hope are, in a sense, bookends. Faith is given us to step out to face hardships and sufferings, but hope pulls us from the future as we are confident that God will work all things together for good (Rom. 8: 28). Our daughter recently played the piano for the prelude to our Lessons and Carols Christmas service. She was nervous, but went ahead in faith. By God's grace, she did well. She was asked to be prepared to play again. Now she has stronger hope that God will indeed take care of her next time as well. Faith and hope work together to see us through the many ups and downs of life.

Let us apply this to our concern for our children. We have hope for the salvation of our children, based in the covenant promises of God. Even if we grieve for a prodigal child, we know God has his timing and plan, and still may hope for the future. Remember Monica's years of prayers and supplications for her wayward son Augustine. We believe God will protect our children from the world and mature them in Christ, and this faith should lead to a definite expectation (hope) that we will see their spiritual growth.

We find the courage to take steps toward these goals when we remember that it is God who works in us…and our children… 'both to will and work for his good pleasure' (Phil. 2: 13). Our desires to help our children come from God, and the energy, perseverance, and hope to take action comes from him as well. The fact that we want our children to be like Christ and are willing to make changes in our lives and approach to parenting and ministry to advance this goal reminds us that God can change our children's wills and actions as well. This hope grows through the hardship of resisting the currents of modern culture and seeking to raise children in a way that honors God. With each little step, our hope grows, just as did my daughter's after she stepped out in faith.

By looking in faith to God, we can take some of the steps we have discussed in the book, having the hope that he will sustain us and work in the lives of our children as well. The powers and principalities are certainly stronger than we are, and it is hopeless to defy them on our own. Given our discussion, I am particularly encouraged by the first two words of that wonderful verse, 'Little children, you are from God and have overcome them, for he who is in you is greater than he who is in the world' (1 John 4: 4). Notice the verb tense: not that we will overcome them, but that we have overcome. The battle is much more inviting when we are told in advance that victory is ours because of God indwelling us. Here is hope indeed!

This brings us full-circle to the truth we examined very early on: we may do things which help or hinder, but it is God the Spirit who works the fruit in the lives of our children. It is his power that will keep them unstained by the world. Faith is our access to this truth, and hope is our knowledge that God will not fail us, nor our children. We therefore cast our cares on the One 'who is able to do far more abundantly than all that we ask or think, according to the power at work within us' (Eph. 3: 20). He is the Almighty God who can change us and our children.

Yes, we must take action and obey, but we do so in faith and hope. God will hear our prayers and use us to minister to our children which, after all, are ultimately his children. He has overcome all the dangers we have described.

The God who raised Jesus his Son from the dead can surely work in the hearts and lives of our children. Reflect with me on Paul's powerful prayer in Ephesians 1: 16–23 as we pray that we will act in faith on behalf of our young people. I pray for you that God will indeed give you a spirit of knowledge and wisdom in the knowledge of God and enlighten the eyes of your heart to know the blessed, certain hope to which he has called you and your children. As we face the rulers and authorities and powers and dominions of this world who threaten our children, may we truly believe 'the immeasurable greatness of his power toward us who believe' as demonstrated in the resurrection of Christ. Whatever the challenges we face, not only do we believe in a God who is infinitely more powerful, but we hope that he will keep our children unstained by the world and cause them to bear much fruit to the glory of his blessed Name.

So, brothers and sisters, hope in God for your children. Seek his face as to how he would have you respond to what we have learned in this study of the Spirit's fruit. Take courage and take action, knowing it is God who has promised and will do it. Share your hope with your spouse, your children, your friends, and your church. Pray together, and work together. We have faith in the certain hope that God is able to keep our children unstained from the world, manifesting the true religion of James 1: 27.

As we finish this book, but step out in faith and hope to minister to our children, join me in the prayer of William Cowper:

> Gracious Lord, our children see,
> By Thy mercy we are free;
> But shall these, alas! Remain
> Subjects still of Satan's reign?
> Israel's young ones, when of old
> Pharaoh threaten'd to withhold
> Then Thy messenger said, 'No;
> Let the children also go!'

When the angel of the Lord,
Drawing forth his dreadful sword,
Slew with an avenging hand,
All the first-born of the land;
Then Thy people's doors he pass'd,
Where the bloody sign was placed:
Hear us now, upon our knees,
Plead the blood of Christ for these!

Lord, we tremble, for we know
How the fierce malicious foe,
Wheeling round his watchful flight,
Keeps them ever in his sight:
Spread Thy pinions, King of kings!
Lest the ravenous bird of prey
Stoop and bear the brood away.

ENDNOTES

Chapter 1

[1] All Scripture references are from the *English Standard Version* (Wheaton, IL: Crossway Bibles, 2001).

[2] Timothy A. Sisemore, *Of Such is the Kingdom: Nurturing Children in the Light of Scripture* (Ross-shire, Scotland: Christian Focus Publications, 2000), 71.

Chapter 2

[1] For all case illustrations, names and details have been altered to make any 'real people' unidentifiable.

[2] Published in 2000 by Christian Focus Publications, Ross-Shire, Great Britain.

[3] This is exemplified by the work recently edited by Benjamin K. Wikner, *To You and Your Children: Examining the Biblical Doctrine of Covenant Succession*, (Moscow, Idaho: Canon Press, 2005).

[4] Christian Smith, *Soul Searching: The Religious and Spiritual Lives of American Teenagers*, (New York: Oxford University Press, 2005).

[5] *Why Christian Kids Leave the Faith*, (Nashville, Tennessee: Charles Nelson, 1992).

[6] Smith, *Soul Searching*, 44.

[7] William Hendriksen, *Galatians and Ephesians*, (Grand Rapids, Michigan: Baker Books, 1979). This section refers to his discussion of Galatians 5.

Chapter 3

[1] *We wish to inform you that tomorrow we will be killed with our families: Stories from Rwanda*, 1998, New York: Picador.

² Ibid., 170.
³ William Hendriksen, *Galatians and Ephesians*, (Grand Rapids, Michigan: Baker Books, 1979), 211.
⁴ 'Current Patterns of Parental Authority', in *Developmental Psychology Monographs*, 1971, Vol. 4, #1, Part 2.
⁵ For example, in his *Authentic Happiness: Using the New Positive Psychology to Realize Your Potential for Lasting Fulfillment*, (New York: The Free Press, 2002).
⁶ This is probably best developed in his *Desiring God: Meditations of a Christian Hedonist* (Sisters, Oregon: Multnomah Press, 2003).
⁷ *Sermons on Galatians*, (Audubon, New Jersey: Old Paths Publications, 1995), 732.
⁸ Ibid., 735.
⁹ Ibid., 744.
¹⁰ Ibid., 755.
¹¹ C.F. Hogg and W.E. Vine, *The Epistle to the Galatians* in *The Epistle to the Galatians and The Epistles to the Thessalonians*, (Fincastle, Virginia: Scripture Truth Book Company, n.d.), 289.

Chapter 4

¹ Søren Kierkegaard, *Works of Love*, (New York: Harper and Row, 1964), 27.
² Ibid., 77.
³ John Piper, *'Love Your Enemies': Jesus' Love Command in the Synoptic Gospels & the Early Christian Paraenesis*, (Grand Rapids, Michigan: Baker Books, 1991), 64.
⁴ See, for example, Rachel Simmons, *Odd Girl Out: The Hidden Culture of Aggression in Girls*, (Orlando, FL: Harcourt, 2002).
⁵ As discussed by Kierkegaard in *Works of Love*, 247.
⁶ Christian Smith, *Soul Searching: The Religious and Spiritual Lives of American Teenagers*, (New York: Oxford, 2005). See particularly 143–5.
⁷ Ibid., 143.
⁸ Source: http: //marriage-relationships.com/divorce_statistics.html.
⁹ William Bennett, *The Index of Leading Cultural Indicators: Facts and Figures on the State of American Society*, (New York: Simon & Schuster), 59.
¹⁰ See, for example, Judith S. Wallerstein, Julia M. Lewis, and Sandra Blakeslee, *The Unexpected Legacy of Divorce: The 25 Year Landmark Study*, 2000, (New York: Hyperion).
¹¹ Ibid., 32.

Chapter 5

¹ Packer, J. I. (1988). *Hot-tub Religion*. Wheaton, Illinois: Tyndale House Publisher. 70.
² Piper, J. (2003). *Desiring God: Meditations of a Christian Hedonist* (2003 Edition). Sisters, Oregon: Multnomah Press.

Chapter 6

[1] Gleick, James. (2000). *Faster: The Acceleration of Just About Everything.* New York: Vintage Books.

[2] Much of this draws from Charles Feinberg's article, 'Peace', in the *Baker Dictionary of New Testament Theology*, Everett F. Harrison, Ed., 1960. Grand Rapids, Michigan: Baker Book House.

Chapter 7

[1] Jean Twenge (2006). *Generation Me: Why Today's Young Americans Are More Confident, Assertive, Entitled—and More Miserable than Ever Before.* New York: The Free Press.

[2] A helpful resource is Marva Dawn's (1989) *Keeping the Sabbath Wholly: Ceasing, Resting, Embracing, Feasting.* Grand Rapids, Michigan: William B. Eerdman Publishing.

Chapter 8

[1] These statistics come from Marva Dawn (2003), *Unfettered Hope: a Call to Faithful Living in an Affluent Society.* Louisville, Kentucky: Westminster John Knox Press.

Chapter 9

[1] Janeway, James, & Mather, Cotton. *A Token for Children.* Republished 1994 by Soli Deo Gloria Publications. Pittsburg, PA, 14.

[2] Wells, David. *Losing Our Virtue: Why the Church Must Recover Her Moral Vision*, (Grand Rapids, MI, William B. Eerdman's Publishing, 1998), 26.

[3] Ibid., 97.

[4] Kilpatrick, William. *Why Johnny Can't Tell Right from Wrong: Moral Illiteracy and the Case for Character Edcucation.* 1992. Simon & Schuster: New York, NY., 90.

Chapter 10

[1] Thanks to my daughter Erin for writing the tale of Frodo and Sam, adapted from the classic works of Tolkien.

[2] Data adapted from Josh McDowells' resources at http: //www.josh.org/notes/file/Internet16-TeenStatistics.pdf.

[3] This story is found in many places, but I take my account from that of Siang-Yang Tan in his recent book, *Full Service: Moving from Self-Serve Christianity to Total Servanthood* (Baker Books, 2006).

Chapter 11

[1] Statistics in this chapter come from *Kid Stuff: Marketing Sex and Violence to America's Children* edited by Diane Ravitch and Joseph P. Viteritti,

Baltimore, (Maryland: Johns Hopkins University Press, 2003) and www.
mediafamily.org, and www.tvturnoff.org.

² See *Kid Stuff*, 135.

³ Ibid., 115.

⁴ See Peter G. Chrstenson's article in *Kid Stuff*, particularly page 116.

⁵ In *Powers, Weakness, and the Tabernacling of God*, (Grand Rapids, Michigan: Wm. B. Eerdmans Publishing Company, 2001).

⁶ In *Evil and the Justice of God*, 2006, Downers Grove, Illinois: InterVarsity Press.

⁷ Published 2004 by Books on the Path, Barker, Texas.

Chapter 12

¹ Source: www.mediafamily.org.

² Ibid.

³ Diane Ravitch and Joseph P. Viteritti (Eds.), *Kid Stuff: Marketing Sex and Violence to America's Children*, (Baltimore, Maryland: The Johns Hopkins University Press, 2003), 125–42.

⁴ Source: Kaiser Family Foundation (www.kff.org).

⁵ Source: www.guttmacher.org.

⁶ Source: www.childtrends.org.

⁷ In *The Disappearance of Childhood* (1994), New York, New York: Vintage Books, 152.

⁸ Italics in the original. *The Death of Character: Moral Eduation in an Age Without Good or Evil*, (New York, New York: Basic Books, 2000), lxiii.

Chapter 13

¹ I should add that this was the information available from the program, and not necessarily the case at the church. Efforts might have been made that were not depicted in this piece. Nonetheless, this is a common enough scenario to make my point.

² 'Teaching amid the Torrent of Popular Culture' (pp. 19–38), in *Kid Stuff: Marketing Sex and Violence to America's Children*, edited by Diane Ravitch and Joseph P. Viteritti, (Baltimore, Maryland: Johns Hopkins University Press, 2003), 26.

³ David Wells, *God in the Wasteland: The Reality of Truth in a World of Fading Dreams*, 1994, Grand Rapids, Michigan: William B. Eerdmans Publishing Company, 222.

⁴ Revised and Expanded Edition, 2003, Enumclaw, Washington: WinePress Publishing.

⁵ Wells, *God in the Wasteland*, 226.

⁶ See, e.g., D.A. Carson, *The Gagging of God: Christianity Confronts Pluralism*, (Grand Rapids, Michigan: Zondervan, 1996). Note especially Chapter 1.

⁷ *Is It a Lost Cause? Having the Heart of God for the Church's Children*, (Grand Rapids, Michigan: William B. Eerdmans Publishing, 1997).

⁸ Ronald J. Sider's *Rich Christians in an Age of Hunger* (20th Anniversay Revision), (Dallas, Texas: Word Books, 1997), is one of many resources to educate you and those to whom you minister about this issue.